The Book of Things

Şeyler kitabı

Also by İlhan Berk, in George Messo's translation

A Leaf About to Fall. Selected Poems †
Madrigals *
Letters & Sound
New Selected Poems 1947-2008 *

* *published by Shearsman Books*
† *out of print*

İLHAN BERK

THE BOOK OF THINGS

TRANSLATED FROM TURKISH BY
GEORGE MESSO

SHEARSMAN BOOKS

This second edition published in the United Kingdom in 2016 by
Shearsman Books
50 Westons Hill Drive
Emersons Green
BRISTOL
BS16 7DF

*Shearsman Books Ltd Registered Office
30–31 St. James Place, Mangotsfield, Bristol BS16 9JB
(this address not for correspondence)*

www.shearsman.com

ISBN 978-1-84861-462-8

Original poems copyright © İlhan Berk, 2002.
Interview with the author copyright © Dilek İçensel and Seçil Yersel, 2001.
Translations copyright © George Messo, 2008, 2016.

The right of İlhan Berk to be identified as the author of this work, and of George Messo to be identified as its translator has been asserted by them in accordance with the Copyrights, Designs and Patents Act of 1988.
All rights reserved.

An earlier version of this translation was first published
by Salt Publishing, Cambridge, in 2009.

The original text was first published in 2002
as *Şeyler Kitabı* by Yapı Kredi Yayınları, Istanbul.

Acknowledgements
Some of these poems first appeared in *Shearsman* and *Turkish Book Review*.

The translator wishes to thank Professor Saliha Paker of Boğaziçi University, Istanbul, for her assistance; Dr Şenol Bezci of Bilkent University, Ankara, for his painstaking revisions, suggestions, occasional puzzlements, and for his unfailing friendship; and Semra Şenol who made the long work of translation endurable and enjoyable.

Contents

Interview with the Author 8

THINGS THAT COUNT THINGS THAT DON'T

things that count things that don't
 Things 19
 Lyre 21

water
 Water, I 30
 I Saw Water, II 33
 Water, III 37

stones
 Stones 40

works & days
 Book of Works & Days 48
 O Diligent Like an Apple 50
 Golden Oriole 52
 Identity Book, Unbelonging 54

four silent texts
 Table 58
 Roundness 67
 ? 73
 Neyzen Tevfik 79

things that count things that don't
 Slug 84
 Tree 88
 Glove 90
 Rubbish 93
 Bra 95
 Mud 97
 Sparrow 102

f	104
Naked Feet	107
Dot / Dash	112
Page/ Paper / Pen	116
sentences I	
Sentences, Here I Come!	124
sentences II	
Night Looks to the East	130
the book / the work	
The Book / The Work	138
Halo	151
Basilica	154

LONG LIVE NUMBERS

I	159
II	198
III	212
summation	245

HOUSE

house I	253
a grand metaphor: house II	259
spirit of the house III	263
house as a family IV	
door	
Door	275
room	
Room	279
window	
Window	282
wall	
Wall I	285
Wall II	287
Wall III	288
Wall IV	289
Summation	290
garden	
Garden	292
little gods of the house V	
Threshold	296
Stairs	298
Ceiling	301
Roof	303
Balcony	304
Notes	307
A Guide to Turkish Pronunciation	308

Interview : *The Book of Things* [1]

with Dilek İçensel and Seçil Yersel

Why the Book of Things: House[2]?

Above all I want to start with the things I've experienced, been intimate with, known. Perhaps that's why the house became a subject. I've said it before in conversation, objects fascinate me. I can't just call paper, for example, *paper*. It's love that binds me to it. I can't simply look on those things I love, like the pens and papers on my desk or any other thing, without feeling. In fact, I personalize them, view them as intimates. For a long time I've wanted to write about the table. It's the same with my study. At a certain time I move into the salon, but such is my relationship that as I leave my study, closing the door, I say "farewell then" to the room. The house is the same. I wanted to write about it because it's a place I've experienced and known.

With this book your adventure, your exploration in writing continues...

First I ought to say that I seldom conceal the workings of the poems or essays that I've written. But if I am to conceal it, it's on the paper to hand I conceal those deeply felt things of use to me in what I've written. Otherwise it doesn't occur to me to hide what I want to say. But it's in the nature of writing, that things get hidden, concealed, obscured, and you see it in this book. Within one vast page sometimes you see three lines, sometimes you find four, sometimes nothing at all. But the very next day you feel you can just about grasp the end of a sentence you looked at previously. At these times, yes, I'm hiding the work, and underlining it in those lines.

Could we read the book as a kind of "Dictionary of İlhan Berk"?

I've never been able to avoid it. I want to put a name to the notebooks in which I've collected my prose, and I imagine it will be called "Auto-I". It's as if there is an entirely separate person living with me and we're both bound to each other in some terrifying way. I want to say that I've never

---

[1] *Şeyler Kitabı* [The Book of Things], Istanbul: Yapı Kredi Yayınları, 2002.
[2] The Turkish word *ev* can mean *house* or *home* (or both simultaneously). The poem *House* comprises Part III of *The Book of Things* and was first published separately by Sel Yayınları, 1997.

been free of my identity. So in some books I've wanted to use things like a "Berk Dictionary". I want to create my own universe. The poet wants to place himself at the centre of reality. That's to say, in a poem, in a piece of writing, I want the writer to be seen. Only then do I feel that art has been made. I want the reader to be with me, to know and to feel as I do. That's when I think the work acquires real meaning.

There's an almost mathematical presence in your poems—would that be true?

In the prose poems I want to impose a visual structure. Let's say I'm typing a piece of writing, when I type I want the text to present a visual appearance too. I once had a mind to write about Süleymaniye Mosque and I wanted the mosque to be present to the reader, even if Süleymaniye itself had ceased to exist. By looking at my text I wanted that structure to emerge. I think I achieved this in my book *Galata*.[3] I covered every square inch of the place in *Galata*..

You say: "In the house everything is there for each other / (confinement requires it)…"

The house is in fact an enclosed presence. But the relationship between those things enclosed together begins there. You enter the house by the door, and thereafter the door extends its proposition to you; it says, look what's happening here. It says there are rooms, sofas, balconies, windows, ceilings. After such an entrance, when you step inside there's a mysterious power. You come up against a wall separating all of this off. The wall suddenly blocks our way and says, yes, there is everything the door says there is but I partition them all. So then I announce to the wall my wish to see a room. Instantly I'm passed through to a corridor. Once in the corridor it begins to ask questions, like where do you want to go. I'll select a room, I say. I come to a door. After we check the door I'm left alone to look for a place to sit. Then I enter into negotiations with the window in order to learn what I can see from the room. The window indicates the nearest spot and from there I begin to look outside. The window is that part of the room containing the greatest freedom. And in the first moment I see the garden, then the street, if the street is visible. But the room is there neither for the window nor for the garden. The room is a freedom unto itself. It's a place in which to dream, to lie down, to sleep or to write. In truth you can't go far in a room.

---

[3] *Galata* [after the district of the same name in Istanbul], Adam Yayınları, 1985.

It has that confinement. So when I say the house's confinement requires it I'm talking about partitioning. There are many partitions inside a house, all there for each other but I want to say that they all live apart from each other too. Their *togetherness* is necessarily an *aloneness* too. And aloneness is in the room more than anywhere else. A room could prolong aloneness to the very end. Between them, stairs, corridors, balconies and sofas establish intimacy but rooms are closed. They form no relation with rooms. I mean to say that stairs, sofas, and corridors form an inner cosmos between themselves. You see, that's how the house fosters both togetherness and confinement.

The question of time and place in your poems…

A poem is written in a time and a place… It's written in a street, on a table, in a house but then there is the question of time. There is a passage between time and place. A poem might be written using a present tense or we might recollect something in the past and the poem pulls us towards the past tense. As the poem is drawn out it brings place along with it. If we leave place out it's as if the poem were in a void. Consider a line that begins "I'm walking…" As soon as we say "walking" the poet wants to know where. Let's say it's a road, a narrow street, the poet wants to write about the street. The street is vital to the completion of the poem. In that case, it's important that time and place are always actively present in the poem. There's no getting away from it. And of course, where it is, where it dwells, when it thinks the things it thinks, are all at work within the poem. The poet has to have a tight grasp on all of this. I generally like to mix times a lot. Then I'm fully conscious of the two times in which I live. And I want the reader to see that too.

The house and death…

At some point in the book I wanted to reconcile the house and death. We live in the house, yes, but it later occurred to me that we die here too. It reminds me of Wittgenstein, one of the greatest philosophers of our time. He learned from his good friend, a doctor, that he was going to die. For a while he'd been living in one hotel after another. "I want to die at home" he said. And that's what the house is—we live there but people must die somewhere and they die at home… I'll never forget, I'd been invited to one of the former socialist countries, I'm guessing it was Hungary, and there was an old man who escorted me around, a poet whose name I forget. "What are you writing?" I asked, and he said "I'm writing about death". That affected me. He was writing an essay on death. "And what are your thoughts on the subject?" he asked. For me it's a word like any other, like *tree, earth, pen*. It doesn't carry the same weight for me. I use it as I'd use any other word.

You say "**the world is something to be learned…**"

Sometimes I meet young people who say "I want to be a poet". I tell them, being a poet will bring nothing but unhappiness. Look, can there be such a thing as wanting to write about the world! I want to write about everything. It's a huge discomfort to me. What else could it mean to write about everything, except to take life away from me? To write about whatever I see or love. I can't just sit on my own and comfortably look at a cactus or an oleander. I look at it as something that must be written about. Such a man's life is a terrible thing, not something to be coveted. The poet is such a man. And for that reason I wouldn't recommend it to anyone. The first thing I say to these young people is: "Poetry is like tuberculosis, like cancer." The poet's life is a kind of hell…

If I hadn't been a poet I'd have chosen to be a cartographer or a greengrocer, or else a ticket inspector on a ferry, like Arif Dino[4]. Cartography became extremely developed in 18th century England. There was a very famous cartographer whose name I can't recall now. Very famous, but seldom one to stray. His wife grew very tired of him sitting from morning to night drawing. One day as he was drawing a map his wife, looking over his shoulder, saw a beautiful village and said to her husband "put down an island there, why not." And momentarily putting aside his responsibilities, there he placed an island. From the 18th century on cartographers searched but could not find that island. Only much later did they learn the truth. That's the kind of map-maker I would have been.

---

[4] Arif Dino (1893-1957): Painter and poet. Brother of Abidin Dino.

THINGS THAT COUNT
THINGS THAT DON'T

things that count things that don't

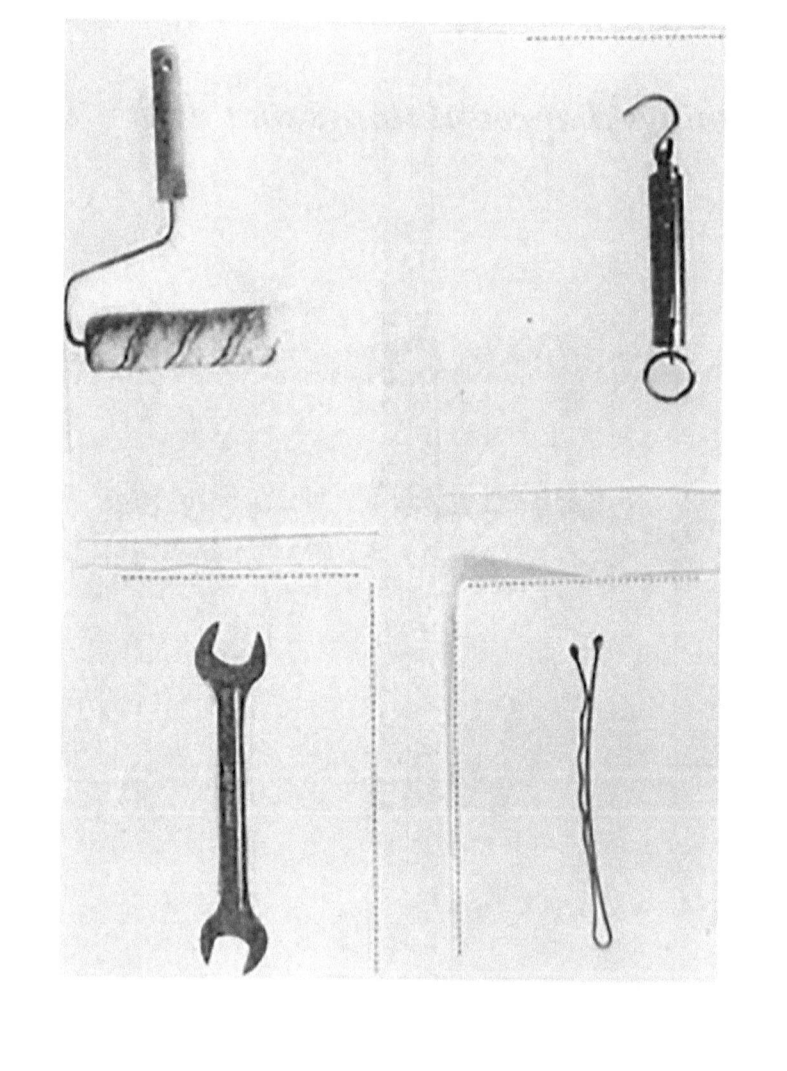

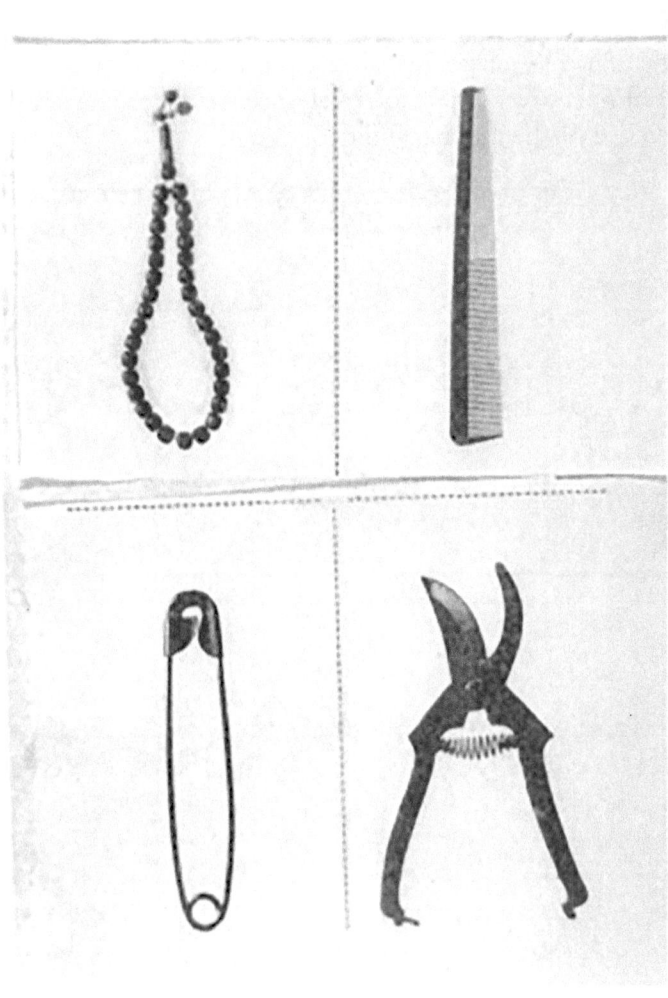

Each thing woke from its sleep.

*

—If objects had language what would you want them to say for you?
—I would want every object to say, all together, "He's one of us".
I have abided by the untouchability of things.

(From an interview)

THINGS

I read things, talkative open gardens.
Tasted the incurability of words, of pencils.

One day I saw
An insect changing place,
                            as if it knew something.

I thought about death's location. The location
Of the cube, the pyramid, the cylinder.

There are no false objects.

Water is the best of things.
Revealing to me the places it saw one night.

I left water with its shadow.
We should investigate its finitude.

Let trees give me a name.

LYRE

> *Thor was getting carried away with the rock's lyre.*
> René Char

1.

To write every poem by demolishing the ones before...
This is writing.

2.

And I've always wanted to try that Chaos, where reality reaches its furthest limits in language, where that relationship between language and *reality's other side* comes to a halt, and how it comes to a halt. Maybe this was just a curiosity. But I tried it. Because I know there can be no talk of poetry if meaning (and reality) isn't overcome.

How is it to live in Chaos, to write of it? This curiosity never left me. To live with the loss of the subject's sovereignty, changing place with the object (even for a short time...)

To set out on such a journey... To draw near to the subject from all sides; but never fully grasp it: only *to circle it*. To start going round again just when you draw near...

3.

    Meaning is seldom grasped in a good poem.
    But it always seems that you've grasped it.
    It doesn't take refuge only in a certain meaning.
    It forms mountain chains like the words of prophets.

4.

    Only poets can never be outside language, no matter how.
    Only language makes hope a reality.

5.

    Emerson talks of the '*fossil poems*' of the language.
    It ought to be called the untouched language.
    The poem's horizon starts there.

6.

    Objects, like images, are given to poets.
    But objects spread fear!
    I always felt this.

7.

    The poem is where the word disappears, the place where it is almost impossible to fix meaning.
    A place, as if not a place.
    Because here language stops speaking.
    It says nothing.
    Sensing, only.

8.

    To write language involves only that:
    Essence is all it needs.

    '*With the inner voice*' (Maurice Blanchot).

9.

   When I finish a poem I view it as if it were not mine. Much later I know it's mine.

   (The sun wants to know where it sinks.)

10.

   Every poem harbours death, violence (violence and writing, one inside the other), darkness.

   (I read that bees collect pollen from among empty flowers.)

11.

    I'm always suspicious of poems I understand.
    I look at the world as images, I see it that way.
    (Like children.)
    Images are my home.

12.

    I could say that it was almost always my aim to rout (*sous rature*) the poem.

13.

>The lyre and the poem are strangers to each other.
>(A distant poem, line of the horizon…)

14.

>Only poets have no hope.

water

WATER, I

I   I am water
     A tiny water.

     A bird is passing.
     I say a bird is passing.

     You hear.

II Every thing
   is so quiet.

   As if in the world
   there was no time.

   Walking around I saw
   myself everywhere.

III I stirred a stone.
A branch,
I rescued from between clouds.

In the world
I talk to waters
that look like me.
(God caught word of it.)

I SAW WATER, II

I   I saw
    water.

    Water
    everywhere
    water.

    Water
    saw
    the face
    of God.

II   Water
the strong.

Water
the virgin.

Water
the feminine.

Water
the race
of Genghis Khan.

III Water
    is smiling.

    Water
    is happy.

    Water
    is joyful.

IV Water
    is returning
    home.

WATER, III

I   *Mevlana says*

    Water says, ask riverbed about stone.

    Stone says, water knows riverbed.

    Riverbed! It will be long. Quiet!

Offering

Dear H_2O

Can I call you a modest,

Vagrant

Old hippy?

stones

STONES

> *… And I will give him white stone and on that stone will be written a name unknown to all except the receiver.*
> GOSPEL OF JOHN

I

Listen to stones,
to what they say,

    most of all.

II

Instantly
stones begin to talk to us,

but they do not know us.

III

Stone
calls stone:

(There is only the named.)

IV

Lean over, look
at the stone;
with both eyes.

Maybe you see a face.

V

Time,

    is time

on stone.

VI

Stones should be touched.
An ethic ought to arise,

from touching.

VII

You should learn
to read stones.

To walk
with them too.

VIII

Does amber
have hands?

Here's a question.

IX

It's doubtful
whether words
can express stones.

I don't know if words know this.

X

Has a paving stone
ever laughed?

—No one knows.

XI

Night,
sleeps in stone.
That's why I carved

you out of stone.

XII

Listen, to stones.
It's voice, of silence.

XIII

Word,
falls upon stone.

Stones,
will always take time.

works and days

BOOK OF WORKS AND DAYS

I opened the learned Hesiod
To see how he wrote *Works and Days*;
While grazing sheep on Helicon.

—He knew but being a poet is a destiny.

Hesiod never left his country
Complaining of Ascra's bad summer
Its difficult winter

Except for a journey by sea.

From roaring Aeolis with
Its rough waves to Luboia,
                              that too.

—Today he is remembered alongside Homer.

O DILIGENT LIKE AN APPLE

*A gift for Arif Damar
at the age of seventy.*

His watch is set to the time of ordinary people, to grass, to insects.
His papers are above rivers, rainbows, and our footpaths.
On his clothes and shoes.
His pages are adjusted to the water's flow.
In their poverty rocks, fires and winds find him next to them.
The one who stands, when houses, markets and streets get up to leave.
O diligent like an apple.
You were a tree among trees.
Left behind in darkness, despised.
You wanted to write whatever there was to write:
Tied in crime.
You wrote.

You know you had a blind friend.
—When he was with you—
He saw too whatever you saw.

Hey dawn, of equal mixture.
The images that are given to poets.
And see the sun is returning from the shore.
How nice your plural face.

GOLDEN ORIOLE

If it's necessary to liken him to the Middle Ages, then he's like one of those medieval travellers with sceptre, sack cloth and a humble face.

Like the prophets he studied the magical language in caves, made friends with Sufis, alchemists, Kabbalists, to foretell the future; he interpreted the Bible according to Iblis; he thought of it as profit, those things poetry had dug from death (poets and death are neighbours), the last traveller.

(You know what I mean.)
Enis Batur.
A poet.
We could also say a petal.
A golden oriole.
A protruding sea.
A monk.
A prophet too.
(Why do I say that?
I don't know either why I say that.)
Maybe the road isn't one we know, it's the one we take.
That's why.
Anyway the road takes its name in the end.
An end that is silence.
Finally he girds himself with silence, hopelessness,
The end, and leaves.
That's what fell to him.

What is it that we call the world?
With its people, trees, birds, slugs.
A book.
Of a thousand pages.[1]
He has been working on this book.

He has taken hopelessness and ordinariness on his croup.

(Hopelessness was there right from the beginning, never will it leave.)

This time he'll find out about ordinariness.

And he knows something else: Poets have no life!

In fact aren't people, animals, a puddle of water, a handful of grass, and insects waiting in single file in the two mouths of the road just to get a place in this book?

But he covets the road.

He sees it.

He's taking it over.

---

[1] For everyone, voluminous, polyphonic: double meanings, remote associations, exits, open-door metaphors, dashes, parentheses, margins, cut-ups, full stops, independent images, blanks, collages, a book with internal-external texts: Sun, eclipses, winds, tides, acid nights, radio nights, loneliness, happiness, unhappiness, propane gas, alcohol, and death....

IDENTITY BOOK, UNBELONGING

1.

Mustafa Irgat walked as if walking in a desert.
He didn't choose that himself.
That's what was given.
He knew that as a way forward.
He stumbled.[2]

It was a poem he chose himself.
Dark, hard, cursed.[3]

---

[2] O weary horse! O temptation!
[3] A network of interlaced paths: A line sets off, taking two lines with it, free-willed. Water ways, ruins… dispersed faces… hands…

2.

No matter how we look at it, his work was an experiment of the indescribable.[4]
As if he was working on a new constitution of fundamental pain and poetry.
That was the real desert.
(Since everything that attains to expression is death.)

---

[4] This, like all other good poets, was his curiosity for the unknown. (He might have been asking whether a book 'can be a vehicle for the absurd'.)

3.

That's why his poetry wasn't out in the open.
Seen only when looked for.
He wrote with the language of silence and invisibility.[5]

His work stays there
An alchemy of '*unbelonging.*'[6]

---

[5] *Some are born to endless night.* (William Blake)
[6] O book openers! O daylight butterflies! O silence! (Let's open up a bracket now for 'Unbelonging' and leave it there…)

four silent texts

TABLE

I

Of all things (in the silent world)[7] perhaps only the table is the clearest, the simplest. Openness, clarity, is the table's basic principle: It resembles nothing other than itself. And reveals itself with its very first breath. And as a word it doesn't contradict its image: It's that, whatever it is: It's never ambiguous. And not only this: it's solid, simple. Its solidity can say nothing other than table. Clarity shines from all four sides of the table. And it throws its entire existence into this: It lives by embracing its name.[8] Perhaps it's through its name that it comes to understand its existence. In fact everything should start this way.

---

[7] The silent world immediately calls out for a bracket. It questions everything: According to whom?

[8] A name-giver. But it doesn't see the name as an unrealized chorus of voices. It behaves like a fundamentalist. A fundamental cynic: He must be saying the opposite of 'I see the horse very well but not the horsemanship.' He says he who sees the horse also sees the horsemanship.

This way we should hold an endless examination of the world of things; we should grasp what is there at our fingertips. Like this we can raise the curtain of another world. Everything has an inner and an outer world: The existence of objects rests in this difference: Existence contains many meanings. It's how it protects its weight. (Suddenly I understand the weight set by the souls of things!) Whereas the table's inner world is set out like this, its outer world is clear too. It can be seen from everywhere. It's not surprising. The table is mostly table from the outside. It's more realistic that way. More itself.[9]

In
brief.

---

[9] We might say a secret liberalist. Its necessity is singular: Happiness. An urgency from birth. Quiet, inward looking. A bit slovenly, insensitive (hair a little long). It places everything before it and lives: without knowledge of secrecy.

II

Table is a privilege: Simple. Brave. Solid. (Simple, because it has no other pieces.) It' not clear why it feels this is necessary. Things also have a life, in their opinion. The table puts this down right at the beginning. Wanted it to be known this way. (Besides, where isn't there privilege?) Maybe this is why it's a fundamentalist. And for this reason also a moralist. (It's in the nature of table to need morals.) Becoming more of a commander. Is it possible that it wanted this? Well yes, and no. But at least it's possible it thought about it. That's certain. Because every table is a personality. It's not easy to say that it likes everywhere. But again, this is a fact: Let's not take up the table and put it just anywhere, for once we put a table somewhere it invades the place immediately. In an instant it's part of that place.[10]

---

[10] When, in a house, you find a place for everything large or small, when you come to the table you stop: Where should the table be put? The table always makes us ask such questions. And it doesn't end there: What will we do with the chair? You see, one more question.

An ordered man likes order. So everything in a room is ordered according to him. An egoist.[11] This needs to be understood. In truth he's a pluralist. Of course, in his opinion. (What isn't opinion?). Once a dinner table, it becomes an activist, its pluralist vein swells at once. It says: *Let no one be left standing!* If it's a writing table, you can't get all that near to it. You can't get close because it's introverted: It lives listening to itself. It talks to itself too. (In a language unlocked only by Kabbalists.)[12]

The table always takes a duty upon itself. An office table has no individual freedom: it's everyone's. The table knows this. It opens its arms immediately and embraces it. The table we're talking about is a little like this. It's for this it works. It's on the table things come together. And can only be thought of and decided on the table. The table is the basis for everything. There is no escape from tables.

---

[11] A commander. Strict. Uncompromising. Can we also say a wise spirit? Silent. Calm. Good.
[12] Its journey is similar to the journey we made under the shadow of death: No more, no less: Sensation deficit: Don't look for meaning! Use it. *Lord of the body, looking down.*

III

What is the nature of table?
Bertrand Russell asks.
Openly, clearly.
Then (as the thing found opposite us):
Four-legged, a rectangle with four wide angles facing each other.
Measured.
Balanced.
Stable.
Stable because it's born that way.
Wooden or metal.
Horizontal.
Horizontal because that's how it will exist.
Solid.
Solid because it's a whole.
It has a form, a depth, a weight.
And like all things it's 'a thing'.
(You know things, they live alone. They don't let anyone interfere with their business.)
And again like all things it has a history.
Harmonious.
Sedate.[13]

---

[13] And perhaps only the table can talk of dignity. So why did we say a moralist?

Table fills the place it's in with magnificence.
You should see it then.
But the table's beauty isn't seen straight away.
We are content with its presence.
And this is enough for us.[14]
Usually we forget about it.[15]
We understand table when we stand over it.
Then we talk with it.
When a book falls from the table:
We both bend down and pick it up together.
We say 'a book fell'.
(Both of us together.)
And the table works concealed inside (like us)
And weaves silence like us.
Exalted silence!
It daydreams in fact.
Tables always do that.
(Its existence requires it.)

---

[14] Actually our interest in objects is nothing more than us wanting to be known, to be understood by them.

[15] Of course the table couldn't care less. Why should it? And maybe tables talk about this forgetting amongst themselves. It's unknown. They say things have no knowledge of sense. In fact everything is alive. This is always overlooked. On the other hand, things don't always use it. And reality doesn't always need to be transparent.

IV

I have an abnormal life with my writing materials as with all other materials. It's endless. And moreover with my table, and almost everything on my table, I talk. Every time I leave the room I say "goodbye". I never once look upon them as mere "space fillers". What is the world anyway but for these things? Every moment, everywhere, we live under the weight of this world of things. Everywhere objects call out to us. This call is something big.
This is why above all else I love my table.
And so it is but for all the love I rain down on my table I'm still afraid to ask if it's pleased with me or not.
Because there's nothing it hasn't suffered at my expense.
It seems to me that I can only ever show my true self, my difficulties, my foul temper, my rudeness, my shabbiness, my instability to it alone.
You see that's why I can't ask.

The Moral

I always had big, long tables, I always worked at big, long tables.
I loaded all of my things on it too. First the dictionaries,
then the real writing materials: Pencil, felt pen, cartridge pens:
Skrips, Parkers, especially Pilot Hi V5, extra fine;
Faber Castell, calligraphy pen 2.0; 20, 30, 50 Rapidos
(you have to hold your hand upright to write, to draw with them,
there's no other way); different kinds of nibs, big small,
especially nibs for hatching (and they are the most beautiful of all
and they draw beautiful lines); different sizes and colours of ink (pelikan),
files (that are always sparking with dreams); pencils that I've gathered from
all over the world, (that never once lose their way); largely Johann Faber, 2200;
Fatih 4B, Schwan; erasers (there's none better than Technics Pro 20s); big and small
scissors, primarily with stainless steel blades; or unknown (since everything is for cutting);
gouache, oils and water colours; different sized brushes; knives, a pocketknife;

(one branded *İlhan of Bursa* always right next to me); Top-Exes,
a lot of Toners (that don't dry or spill easily); cut and left, coloured writing
papers
with or without writing on; two nail files size big and small;
a Sony hand radio; a huge, white and blue, beaded plate
(for drying fruit); a Baby Hermes typewriter (we're almost the same
age); thick, thin javelin pens; razors, rotrings blue azure,
deep red, weiss white, brown maroon; glues, staplers, post-it notes 3m.;
rulers (pioneering the line), pins, drawing pins,
book marks etc… And what about my pipes, my tobaccos (once upon a
time
I had my hands on them all the time, but these days maybe once or twice
I rarely hold them now), aren't they still part of the table's inventory,
and only the table's? Doesn't it hold the writing's hand, who could say
the opposite? On the other hand, because I work at three different places,
on three tables, if not all, then can't most of them be replicated?

ROUNDNESS

Do you know roundness?
Who doesn't?
Where doesn't the eye see it, distinguish it, and is then arrested by it?
Locked inside the world of things, immanent. What could be more natural for an object? It will retreat far into itself and look out from there. It will keep all that it sees to itself, share it with no one, burying in its closed world as with all others of its kind.
Is it destiny?
Destiny too is something like this. Because it chose itself, it expects nothing at all from the world. And of all things what could be more introverted than the circle itself?
A concealed realist.
Esoteric.
On its door hangs a huge sign saying: No Entry!
Like a circle it starts from one point and again comes back to it, placing itself in a hoop.
An Aristotelian.

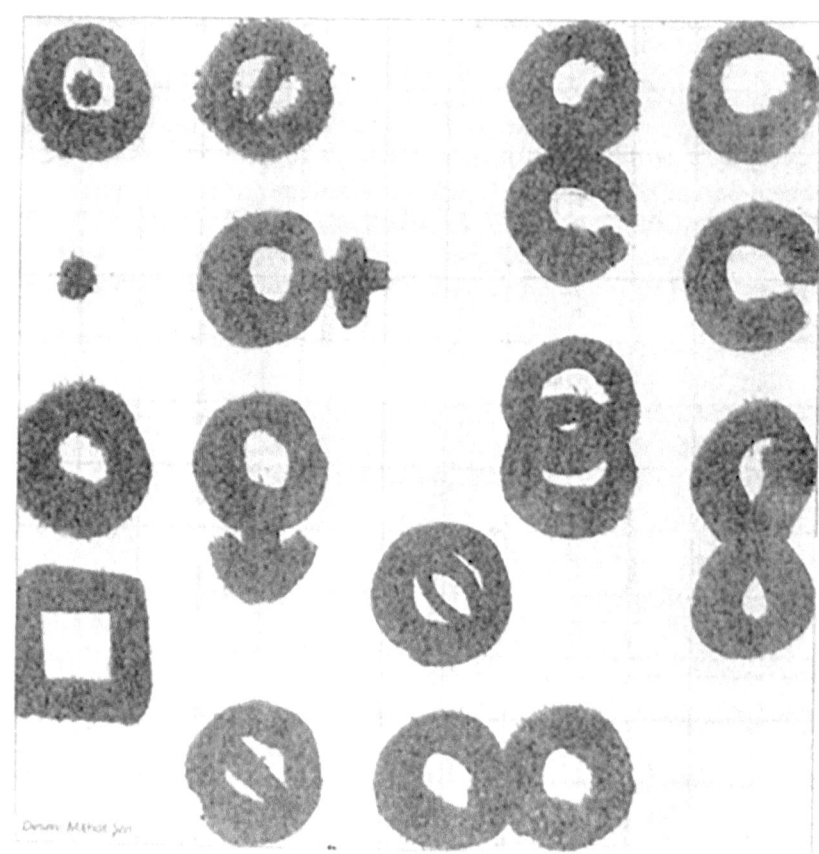

That's the way it is, but we can't really say that roundness excludes the external world: Because life is round. Still, if there's something it does exclude, it's geometry. The circle rejects geometry's domain. (It does its best not even to recall its name.) It embraces everything. Without ever changing. Don't we see its various outward forms everywhere? What else could assume a thousand and one forms like this?

There's nowhere its imperialism doesn't extend, as it wraps itself around iron, stone, wood, glass and soil: Forever taking its place next to us in the form of a plate, a spoon, a vase, a clock, a chair, a mirror, a glass, a lamp, a cupboard, a table, a globe, a ball etc… A chameleon! It appears too in everything we eat and drink. Eggs, onions, garlic, potatoes, cauliflowers (dear cauliflower), celery, cabbage, turnips, melons, grapes, watermelons.

There's nowhere it doesn't place or stretch a hand or leg. It's a townsman, mainly. A captain of industry. Its influence continues everywhere. It turns its back on geometry too and laughs.

It turned the world upside down by turning into a wheel.

And so inscribed speed on earth (how should speed be explained, this contemporary dynamo?). And only speed? Didn't it also teach us silence (silence is a revolution too)?

And roundness itself is its content. (Geometricians have never yet perceived the true essence of roundness, limiting themselves to its outer edge. They never really thought of its inner space as something full, beyond the limits of reason. They recognize the world as something flat, empty. As if its essence had been discarded. As if they had said understanding isn't our job. It's doubtful they even know we live inextricably with roundness.) Roundness is an atlas of meaning. It can be seen from all sides, it is beyond our imagination.

Difficult to read like an atlas too. And if we follow Jaspers: Every presence conceives of itself as round. The natural state of roundness is necessarily internal, not external. (It is unique to us to experience the surface superficiality in everything.) What is it that's empty inside? Emptiness also has a language, a meaning, like fullness. Like all of us it's conscious of it too. As a shape on earth (such as roundness), no other shape can convey the sense of touch, the play of our hands on it. Whatever shape it assumes, it becomes life itself. Closed, yes, tight-lipped but its nature requires it. Secretive too. It has to think and solve everything on its own. It closes its windows and lives like that. (Place all the round, secretive objects there are in the world before your eyes, and think!) No one can complete with roundness: it assumes forty appearances: it makes no concessions, but it's no bigot. It knows how to break out of its shell when necessary. By breaking into a thousand pieces (of course whoever did escape with their identity intact?) it adopts and takes on a thousand different shapes. As if giving the first examples of the art of puzzle-making. But not like a Gestalt theorist, entering into the order, the nature of its own world, following its own mark: but as the handle of a cup, the decorative frame of a window, a clock's allure, everything on a surface (as a full-stop, a footnote in a piece of writing)…

Despite its allure we can't really say it's been liked. But like some people: we can't rigidly say "An object should know how to be loved, and if it doesn't, then that's its problem." I, for one, can't do it.

Roundness, as a word, never stirred the curiosity of poets. It starts with R and ends in S. As if for poets it incurs no meaning. Two celled. Nor is it a word you can articulate in a single breath. For the O (one of the vowels of roundness) you need to stick out the lips, like this:

ROUNDNESS.

Are we therefore going to shake it and throw it around? Besides, everything requires a bit of effort; roundness too (as a word) has a right to ask this. Anyway, it's not true that roundness has some kind of deficit of meaning:

    a) in the language of philosophy it's a symbolist
    b) special to psychology
    c) a rationalist in geography
    d) an intellectual in history (we could say the first Kantian)

In point of fact it's the foundation of the most beautiful sentences:

THE WORLD IS ROUND!

And isn't it, when all is said and done, the halo of our love? Who could not, with all its sincerity, feel it close to them?

What would Freud (poet of our souls, soon to be emperor) have thought about symbols, I wonder?

Particularly about the question mark? Paul Steinberg surprises us by comparing the question mark with the exclamation mark. He can't stand to see the question mark's head downcast, is furious at its weakness in the face of the exclamation mark (he resents its selfishness, its looking down from on high). He's not entirely unjust, for asking questions is a kind of rebellious duty and yet the neck bends in submission. It's not something we can easily understand of course. Which is why he says: "*The question mark arouses suspicion*".

When you compare the question mark to other forms of punctuation, in terms of its essence and shape, it's like no other.[16] An independent spirit. And it isn't unique only of its kind: it is singular in the history of things, alone (so long as we don't count the oblique headed screw, the swan, and so on). But why wouldn't it look like an ear?[17] And not only in form but in content (it opens its ear to all sounds like an amplifier)? And isn't this their reason for existing anyway?

---

[16] Punctuation's other members?
Full-stop, comma, darling bracket,
inverted commas, dash, quotation mark, exclamation mark,
colon, ellipsis, and so on.

[17] At least like my ear?
In the mirror it says: "I'm straightening you!"

It's a question mark but never wholly sated with just questioning, it waits for the answer, wants it. It is mainly a rationalizer (one that sees reality with all its contradictions). And seeing how it pokes about for the ins and outs of everything why shouldn't we call it a dialectician, or even a Hegelian? The dictionary definition: 'A thing given meaning.' To give meaning. To look for a meaning in everything: It's really insistent about this. And more often than not, it assumes a form like this:

Both a question and an exclamation. Because it will form an adverb. Only to be a question, to create questions suddenly wasn't enough. In fact what else could be more important than a question?

Yes, it's introverted, compared to the exclamation mark's boisterousness, its clamorousness. Yet even as it becomes introverted it assumes a function: it takes hold of polysemy's hand—polysemy, without which the act of writing (this gangrene) is nothing. But not only this, by adopting different forms (word, adjective, pronoun, etc…) like all of us, it keeps on doing its marvellous job. Which of its species has this? If we exclude the comma, which of them is as swift, as dynamic?

It was the full-stop, the bracket, the exclamation (these writing demons which smother everything [let's keep counting them] quotation mark, star, square bracket, extension, break, and so on) all working to stall and foreclose the act of writing as soon as they can.

They are the true monuments to stability, to introversion. They see nothing except themselves. Full of self-importance.

On the other hand, when the question mark is compared to its partisans it's like movement itself. And why shouldn't it be remembered: the line of motion is curved. And because it knows the necessity of its nature, it looks around with its head held high. At least it isn't at all offended by its bending, and doesn't say I bow in humility. But it's as if the question mark were not only the shape of movement but of existence too. In the history of things it has a picturesque beauty.

It holds the hand of writing sincerely, with love. Who has the same magnificence, who, the swagger? Modern Art opened new pages for it like a duvet. Actually, it can't be written with the same ease as a full-stop, a comma: You hold the pen as if drawing one circle within another, then suddenly you go down and put the full-stop. Of course it isn't easy. But what beautiful thing doesn't require this kind of difficulty? Isn't it the most beautiful thing on this page?

Yahya Kemal reworked the question mark seven times in 'Gök Kubbemiz'. And don't we find the very best version of it in his hand writing?

And what about Ahmed Haşim? Didn't he leave us little *Piyale*, framing it in seven different question marks? And we know it's the full-stop side by side that he's smitten with, that he loves most of all. Not counting "Hasta Çocuk" from *Rübab-ı Şikeste*, then it's as if Fikret never used the question mark. So be it. We can't despise him for it. Isn't it well known he didn't change the exclamation mark or the semi-colon for anything? Perhaps its shape didn't interest him, or its meaning. It's difficult to know. Even if he wasn't a friend to the question mark, he wasn't its enemy either.

The Moral

No matter how much you write about symbols, it's never enough. Alphabets, numbers, notes, signs, hand writing (the overlord of symbols); this silent world of indicators that adopts a myriad of different shapes, so making everything the subject of signs. And so every property is a sign. (Doesn't Foucault say 'The alphabet is a trader'?) Didn't we say the symbol is a founder of passwords, a sceptic? Well, it's a sceptic, a founder of passwords. But how can they not be sceptics? In the name of reality they check everything and thus they achieve inertia, right?

It's a difficult life!

NEYZEN TEVFIK

When I saw Neyzen Tevfik sitting on a Fatih Park bench (his childhood next to him, his cat, his panther, yes, panther, and Barbaros conqueror of the seas), looking at Mount Fuji, at the same time I found myself sitting there between them staring at the same Mount Fuji. In the mountain's hem, the world's first residents, ants, along with bees, were going about their tasks. Right behind them an uncharted island, an area of darkness and Lake Lut were slowly coming into view. They were also watching a puffed up rooster, a child of fifty-three, bats, a camel-load of Damask silk, a hill called Friday, a river pouring loneliness from top to toe, an insomniac night. (How strange, the sky we know as sky wasn't there.) I saw all of this and I didn't see it. Above their heads a simple orchestra of grasshoppers, flocks of birds, cicadas, and the poet of poets Bashō approaching.

>   And a bashful triangle
>   and the soul of animals
>   and the loneliness of a three-storied house
>   and a child-sun
>   and a shadow unmoving from its place
>   and a thorny braided wire
>   and a lame reason
>   and speckled water
>   and the letter Z.

Cihat Burak.
tuval üzerine yağlıboya, 1975

II

I took out a pen and paper, took Neyzen who had stopped looking at Mount Fuji, and started drawing his picture. He put on white clothes (I love white clothes, I dirty the white a little, I dirtied it). The panther was staring at Mount Fuji. I choked the panther and Mount Fuji in black. The cat understood everything: He stood to attention and struck a pose (the cat wasn't from our neighbourhood, I know all the cats). It brought forward its legs. It hardened its stare. It stretched out its whiskers. And stuck its tail out more. Pricked its ears too. Everything became stone and the waiting began. A man in the mouth of a street with jonquils and sand lilies in his clothes began to shout out 'Burnt Sienna, Black-White Genoese, grey Paris, colourful Florence, golden Venice!'

(Mount Fuji had stopped erupting [where is Mount Fuji?] and was taking a rest.
And with it tall sea-tongued boys,
Bearded bird,
Children…)

III

Neyzen was bored, stood up and took his coat from behind him. I gave his coat from behind. He was holding his ney in his right hand. I drew him with his right hand holding the ney. He put his left hand on his left knee. So I took his left hand and placed it on his left knee. He sat there wearily. So I sat him wearily down. His right knee was slightly raised. I raised his right knee slightly. He left his curly hair uncombed. I left his curly hair uncombed.

(For flowers and kids and birds to pull it down.) His shirt was yellow. I left it yellow. He'd opened the front of his jacket. I opened it a little. His trousers were pulled up to his waist. I left them pulled up to his waist. All four of his four buttons were showing. I made the four visible buttons visible. When he sat he pulled up his trousers. (His trousers were taking a rest, as they might in a painting in an easel.) I pulled them up and made him sit. He turned his right foot a little to the right. I turned his right foot a little to the right. His left foot he kept straight. I kept it straight. Ten toes of his two feet were showing. I left them so they'd show. He turned his face to me. So neither of us would be bored I turned it a little to one side. His mouth was neither open nor closed. I left it like that. Only his right ear could be seen. Only his right ear showed. His dark eyes were dark. They stayed dark. However an apple sits on a table, that's how he sat. I left him the way he was. A dark shadow fell across his face, and I left it like that. Down below, miserable birds were perching and flying back to Mount Fuji. I left them like that.

I went further down and looked, I came closer and looked. Everything was exactly the same, unchanging, in a constant cycle of change.

Unchanging, they remained in a constant cycle of change.

things that count
things that don't

SLUG

I

From out-
    side it looks as if it inscribes a circle but when time comes to close back in from whence it came suddenly it retracts both ends of the line and darts inside.
    A bungalow.
    Spherical.
    Shape of shapes.
    You see it resembles nothing other than itself.
But if we must compare it to something, then let's say a restless water drop.
(Armoured, solid, luminous)
    In a shell as thin as a membrane and so strong, transparent
    A spiral
    Alluring.[18]
When you touch its shell with your forefinger:
—Ping!
you'll hear a sound. Or
—Crack!
when it's broken.
    When you take it and look at it in your hand you'll see it creates a spiral bandage which wraps its beautiful shell like a ball.
    (Fast growing and discarded.)

---

[18] Didn't William Blake call you 'holy'?

But still, think of it as a dark well.
Or a bottomless well.
One you can descend into but never get out.
Or we could call it a clever puzzle.
(Existence is dialectical.)

(Whenever I, the weak, try to draw that sphere hasn't it always stumbled and fell?)

Didn't it get that shape anyhow after a long and arduous journey?

For this introverted curved line (crookedness props up the world) didn't it wrangle with geometry?

A small world.

Solid.

Dark.

II

From in-
 side, then we'll start from the shell's mouth, from that intractable place. From that place, according to botanists, where it beds down for its winter sleep, from where it turns and twists its form from top to midriff.
 Isn't everything there?
 Lungs (they almost take up all the space), heart (which is a slug itself), bogey-rag (it being the bogey-bug, we know it owes its existence to it, or at least to its clumsiness, slugs are clumsy), intestines (stretching from one end to another), vagina (always at the ready), anus (sensual), brain (with its cover not opened yet), tongue (that comes and goes), tentacles (always at the ready, and isn't that where its eyes are?) etc.
 It will look from there at this place we call the world: Retracting its antennae, purveying every inch of the ground it passes, with one foot slowly (slowly? In one minute it can cover 1.12m–1.85m) it will raise its home on its back and traverse a continent.

(I wonder if it's doing exactly that while I'm writing this?)
Then let's leave it, let it crawl on through!

Offering

Tell me, slug, do you love me?

Dear slug, you are one of my many loved, despised, strange, pitiful residents; for how long I have wanted to write about you, how often the pen came to my hand only to fall from it, the paper sliding away—today is destiny. When I started this I believed I would write about you better than all the other insects. (Perhaps it's because we've known each other for so long or because of the special love I have for you [special, yes, but I still haven't fathomed it].) I carried this consuming wish within; you can't imagine how overjoyed I am that I can do this now. Overjoyed because like all the many creatures that come into my little house and follow me from place to place, on my pens and papers, you're one of my friends; and now you appear among my commonplace writings.

How could I not be overjoyed?

Farewell.

TREE

I'm the tree.[19]
A tree
unlike any other you've seen in the world.
There is nothing at all to compare them.
Not even two drops of water are alike.
This world tries to make me other than I am.
Still it's me.
Another me:
A tree's shadow.
Nothing is clear anyway.
'Should we dwell in the moment, or beyond it?'[20]
Or should we disappear?
It's this I don't understand.
And everything is one vast silence.[21]
I see a bird passing by.
A river widens where it pools up.
I only look to things.
Looking is my job, only to look.

---

[19] A picture of a tree; in time and space. (Oil on canvas 69 x 40cms, 1969), Devrim Erbil.
[20] When you exist, to not exist. But not exactly that: everything loses blood.
[21] In fact everything has a meaning. There isn't anything without meaning.

Everything in the world I miss like mad.
Everything I had was a small garden.
I can never forget the houses and streets and sky that could be seen
    from there.
Now there is no one [22]
I never thought to be a tree in a painting.
Not counting my roots (I can't see my roots either)
There hasn't been a big change.
No one can say I'm not alive,
As if I were on a long, long journey.
I'm endlessly extending,
But this isn't eternity.[23]
But I know I'm caught up with eternity.
It's out of my hands, and I find my situation strange.
To be in the world in a painting…
That's all.
It must be something like this:
To exist.

---

[22] In this world I'm like an empty sack. As if I'm bargaining with death.
[23] I'm continuously flowing: I can neither be nor not be.

GLOVE

Always
you are
the glove
when I'm
a hand

While
hand offers
openness,
glove
closes it

Gloves
carry
you
every-
where.

The glove
forever
provokes
the hand,
deletes itself.

No one can stop thinking about the hands of Halil Pasha's women, those who wore gloves.

A
sorcerer
a
magician.

When
the glove
stays
in the raincoat's
pocket
—it's you
who stays.

It's a victim,
it chose
to be
a victim.

It adores
this maturity.

RUBBISH

Thing that once had an identity, was once useful, a thing suddenly robbed of usefulness, stripped of its identity:

Rubbish.

That's how rubbish is.

Can't stand on its own two feet like a lamp, a chair, a table, a rock etc. (rocks stand up on their own), stupefied, cannot be saved from constant change, metamorphosis
a pitiful thing.

It has no colour, no shape and yet comes and goes in all the shapes and colours there are; it takes on every form, every shade.
An alloy.
One that's seen everywhere, is unavoidable, sticks to our feet, is thrown away, kicked about, despised:

Homeless and rootless.
That is, but shouldn't be.
Dog-like.
Cursed.

(Does it say 'The world is full of demons'?)

Like all other things it's silent, serious minded (serious mindedness, silence are particular to things; gradually they form a family:

A family of things that do not count).

That's the way it is, but a snapped button, an old slipper, a handkerchief, a sock are magical.

Like all objects too it's attractive, haloed.

An ascetic.

A melancholic.

(Besides, rubbish and a melancholic aren't such different things: They're like each other.)

With the soul of a monk.

Empirical.

Expects nothing of this world.

As if, like Diogenes, it says "I ask only that you leave no shadow."

A metaphor.

Acrid.

(Isn't the world a metaphor too?)

Rubbish is lyrical.

BRA

A magical, sensual jewellery box in the history of things: the bra.[24]

If you ask its neighbouring words like brace, bracelet, or bracken (o beautiful rustling bracken) they'll call it ordinary, unimportant, a meaningless word.[25] Yet few words are as enticing, sexual, alluring.

It goes far beyond the object it names, it posits only its own being, presses it forward, emphasizes.[26]

It uses only provocative, sexual pathways and labyrinths.

It thrusts out from there.[27]

---

[24] Why shouldn't we call it the innocent Eros?
[25] Words breed meaninglessness. And they use that meaningless as they see fit.
[26] Isn't it breathless and consumed with the fire of its own kibla?
[27] It craves abandon in moments of dizzying ecstasy.

As if it sought intoxication, wanting to live and die intoxicated.
Happy like that.
And why not?
Besides, the object of happiness is darkness.[28]
It lives with the great dream of the body.[29]

---

[28] It defies description. Is unknown. Incomprehensible.
[29] It grew up in caves, came and went with orgasms and little deaths.

MUD

I

Mud, a name.
And like all that have names it has a history.
From a silent world.
(The silent world is our real world.)
And like all objects, an object.
Yet it has no definite form.
It sleeps on the floor.

It only has a face.
The face of mud, its only form.

Like all other worldly things it lives by retreating into itself.
From the earth's surface, yes.
A gru.
It's there with the earth:
The way it thinks of itself on the earth, that's how it finds itself.

It's as if it was never ashamed to be mud.
To be was enough perhaps.
It just wanted a place, like everything else.
It was overjoyed to find itself the soil on a road.
It expected nothing more than a simple life.
And it got it.

II

Everything looks a little like something else, but mud resembles nothing.

Everything can be compared with something else, but mud can't be compared with anything.

Everything in this world has a use, but mud is useless.

Everyone has someone in the world, but mud has no one.

III

Mud is unlovable.
And why?
Nobody knows.
Maybe because of its name.
(It starts off slandering until it's up to its neck in filthy jobs.)
Ok but, what's this to mud?
It's not that simple just to call mud, mud.
It has a place in the world, like all of us.
And like us too it has a name.
Is it such a small thing to have a name?
Knowing this alone ought to be enough for us.
Everything has a certain immunity.
But not mud.
Wherever we see it, we step over it.
Its very existence is almost unbearable for us.
And yet, like other common things, mud is mysterious.

Offering

Look, have a good hard look at mud: You'll love it! Everything has a
    personality.
I lived with things that do not count as much as others that do.
By entering into the writing of someone like me, mud enlarged me.

  O passers-by!
  Be sparing, don't hurt the mud.

SPARROW

Of all the names perhaps the names of birds, streets, and trees are the most beautiful.[30]
Especially bird names.
Counting only those that begin with 'a' would be enough.
Beginning with Albatross, Anhinga, Ash-throated Crake.
But there are none better than those starting with 's':
Swift, Snipe, Saffron Finch, Sanderling, Spotted Sandpiper
And especially the quickest to say: Sparrow.[31]
Which bird is as tender, as beautiful?
But the sparrow's real beauty comes from its modesty, from its ordinariness.
And ordinariness is its true self.[32]
It passes its time with thrown-off things and yet it does not sacrifice its pleasure (yes, its pleasure) for anything.[33]

---

[30] Names are voices. We know them by sounds. Letters are the shadows of names. People can't do without names, and will name no matter what.
[31] Who doesn't know the sparrow? Two syllables but as if they were one. Who first gave the sparrow its name, I don't know. But I'd like to know what the sparrow thinks of it.
[32] Is it easy to be ordinary? And not only that: which bird is content with its name, its reputation?
[33] It's no small issue being in this world.

Finding the vault of heaven silent, it fills it with its chirp chirp.
Like Buddha it doesn't yearn for things that don't belong to it.
And again like Buddha it is silent. Contented.
Content because it wanted only to be a sparrow: and it is.
A sage. (Birds and sages are alike.)
Beautiful. Round-eyed. Merry.
And with light brown feathers.

It doesn't complain.
Admires nothing.
It's just like a horse. (Horses don't admire each other.)
Doesn't ask "Where am I?"
It's there.
A little silly, a little daft.
Of rabble nature. (Who isn't?)
But in truth, unhurried.[34]
A consummate humanist.[35]
As you'll see, with a half-monk, half-Brahmin soul.
It goes everywhere with hop hop tiny steps. (And why should it hurry?)
And like all of us, it believes in love and death.
And again like all of us, it learns by doing.
Thanks, sparrow.

---

[34] Unhurried because it has no possibility of knowing what it has not lived.
[35] It sits with me at the courtyard table (God thought up courtyards for birds). And again it rises with me.

Is it the alphabet's most beautiful letter?
f, for sure.
(The small letter, as if I didn't know the capital.)
The tallest.
The naughtiest.
The most delicate.
The most magical.
(Did we also say the most childish?)
The most latent.
The loneliest.

Why the loneliest?
I don't know this either.
Maybe *f* likes to hide.
Perhaps it finds loneliness very humanistic, that's why.
And this:
Loneliness is what the alphabet shares in common.
Some were born that way.
And *f* is conscious of its loneliness.
Like poets, it sees this as its fate.
Otherwise who would want loneliness?
Every letter has a character.
And the power of movement.
The power of letters is terrifying.
And again whenever loneliness is the subject perhaps *f* dreams itself as an island.
Or a labyrinth.
Anyway, it's everyone's right to dream.
The truth is all letters want to hide.
Especially *f*.
But to me, I compare *f* to you, like our chaotic meeting here on this earth.
Isn't that where it washes up in this piece of writing?

U

uuuuuuuuuuuuuuuuuuuuuuuuuuuuuuuuuuuuuuuuuuuuuuuuuu
uuuuuuuuuuuu
uuuuuu

u[36]

---

[36] A penniless man riding a horse in Dicle.

NAKED FEET
(An object that momentarily lost its subject)

> *...many a gift*
> *Comes to me on these naked feet.*
> Paul Valéry

I

Bare feet are an open invitation.
Nakedness is almost a reason to exist.
They project themselves, starting from a love-like tryst.
For nakedness is their only gift.

II

As conveyors feet don't exist unless naked.
That's why we don't see them.
They don't come out.
They secretly withdraw.
They know that they exist.
Nakedness doesn't just arouse feet sexually and leave them:
It consecrates them.

III

A dream land: Naked feet.
Seductive, perverting, fearless.

Thus begins their dizzying journey.

IV

They need to be looked… looked at… looked at…
(To look is to seduce)

The feet,
Are there for such a gift.

V

Island in the geography of the body.
White doves!
(I always think of them between sheets, the glimmering ankle half-out.)
Female.
They thrive on sensation.

(The ankle needs a eulogy.)

VI

In the language of feet, touching is love.
And this, for one whose world is to look, is equal to death.

VII

Bare feet say:
—Let me not
be lonely, without dreams.

VIII

For feet, there is no happiness except in being naked.
Their deepest state is nakedness.

IX

> *I looked at that body.*
> Cavafy

The foot is a part of the body but this changes nothing.
(Every whole is both part and whole.)
Who awakens, inflames, arouses the body?
What wouldn't bare feet say?
It's been forgotten that feet talk.
Feet are more naked, more sexual than all the body's other parts.

I see your red heel (darling sorcerer), I love your foot.

That's you.

DOT / DASH

I

So here are two words with a lot to say:
Dot and Dash.
Dot was unloved right from the start.
Even Euclid doesn't want that word in his mouth.
'A thing without breadth' it says.
(But only breadth? It has no shadow. Let's say that too.)
There's nothing surprising in that.

A rationalist, a dictator, a commander.

But essentially an enemy of imagination: It starts off by wringing the neck of a beautiful word or sentence. Half way through it puts up barricades and makes a blockade of everything.

It finds the journey of creation tedious and wants to cut it short. And in this way does it squeeze the life from the act of writing, freeze it and leave it for dead.

But its insistence, its arrogance finds no entry into modern works: For page after page the shadow of a dot never falls.

Pythagoras would call the dot the First Being.

First and last.

II

There's no journeying with a dot.
The dot stays still as stone.
Knows no increase.
Arrogant, selfish.
Semiotics' most bigoted member: Hangs a sour face to the whole family, turns up its nose.
Regards the comma especially as an enemy: If it could, it would wipe it out entirely.
And yet who has the richness of a comma? It is, above all, a journeyman: There's nowhere it hasn't been.
It is ready to compete with time and space. What more could one ask?
The dot is an enemy of detail. It doesn't know that everything is in the details; it doesn't want to know. Maybe that's why it's angry with the comma.
Who know?
But of course no one loves the oppressor.
But that's how it is, eternity's vanguard (for some poets eternity is everything, while others turn their noses up at it!) It holds the hand of dash. And it's great.
And the dash does well in coming after dot, it finds its place wherever dot's shadow falls. Who wouldn't want that?

III

The dash is formed by a walking dot.

(Dots walk.) And the dash's nature is to gird on distance, like zero. Only distance? Future too. (Like eternity, the future has no beginning, no end.) No sooner was it created then it was shared. And so it isn't slow to take up its unique position in the history of things. On the other hand, it's the symbol of negativity: It carries its identity as a separator, a divider. When we compare it to dot (we can't compare it but) it's wrong in every respect. Unlike the dot, dash's being can't be tethered. It stretches out as fast as it can. It clears away anything in its path. (The history of speed should be documented.) It's self-propelling. It dons a variety of shapes but first it assumes the shape of an arch (dear arch) and sets off around the world, from one end to another. But not before calling in on Euclidian Geometry: It will step out with parallel and diagonal lines, with squares, climb with triangles, drop down into open-closed spaces. And in this way it tries out every possible shape before finally waking up to itself. As a dash, it's always on the go: as if it was looking for itself. (Doesn't everything have a past, a present, and a future, and one that it will live through?) And that's what it is to be a dash.

PAGE / PAPER / PEN

I

Paper says, let me not be tainted, dirtied.
Paper is silence.
It tells nothing.

Is meaningless too.

It spreads fear of enclosed emptiness.

•

(Closedness is paper's nature.)

II

White paper is love.

Pen and paper were made for such a relationship.

Every word takes up its dictionary place like this,
And is aware of it:
Tree, the word for tree;
Death, the word for death.

III

You're the page, always.
It sees you.

'Your skin imparts the feeling of paper'
says the sage

•

I say, caress it, talk to it,
Before it puts on its clothes.

IV

The page is damned.
It reads the unknown, syllable by syllable.
Draws it to the field of merciless 'non-existence', then abandons it.
Only to choke it, right in front of it.

•

Pour, empty the load of your name here, it says.
The word isn't a thing.

V

The word "pen"—you say—doesn't look like a pen.
Pen writes:

> I = Other
> Other = I

VI

A voice said 'In three days I fill my bin, I'm wasting a ton of paper.'

The paper was grinning.

VII

Paper,
Is an invitation to travel.

It envelopes eternity.

•

To write is to journey from word to word.

Offering

Thanks to you brother pen.
Dear page.
Beloved paper.

Thanks to you.

sentences I

SENTENCES; HERE I COME!

I

    Somewhere I remember saying 'with sentences I learned about the world.'
    The world is sentences.
    I never want to miss this spectacle.

II

…to tread the outer limits of impossibility—it says…
…to walk there…
    To look and call out from there…

III

   Sewers, silk roads, death beds, naked balconies, perverted clumsy (endless) phalluses, unfalling guillotines, lizards walking a rope…

   (Thus rashly do sentences compete with each other.
As if speed was everything to them.)

IV

   Shamans talk about life,
   Lamas talk about death.

   That's what I read.

V

Once, I found sentences talking to each other.
Sentences are alive.

VI

Sentences establish no interest in us.
Why should they?

VII

A sentence said I share your anxieties (from where it dwells, like a marginal note).

VIII

Sentences see more of the other
than we can

IX

    Human beings are secret.

X

    Let's turn from the unknown
    To the known.

sentences II

NIGHT LOOKS TO THE EAST

I

…sentences began with Syrian merchants.
Much later I opened a window facing the river.
A wounded woodcock came in.

I woke to the sounds of rough Latin.

II

 We fell from the middle of a book, medium-sized sentences in search of our place, in a city we didn't know (for the city's name was nowhere to be seen) all through the night we wandered. It looked like London, but it wasn't, that's for sure; how could we be so sure? Nowhere did the Thames bridges suddenly appear; no Oxford Street, no Hyde Park; it looked like Istanbul but it wasn't Istanbul; it could have been Venice, Amsterdam, canals everywhere, water, everything living on water, but it wasn't; maybe Baghdad, Delhi, Peking; the three of us kept our eyes to the floor and didn't speak; but fireflies, birds, playing cards, ants, suspension bridges, Carthage—yes, Carthage—dinosaurs, dogs, water ways, sewers, water flies and bandages all caught around our ankles and kept stopping us and still we couldn't find our place on pages.

 Maybe our existence was prescribed.

 We were cast off.

III

    We were in a Palace of Delights, then moved to a House of Dotage.

IV

    I'd undress you.
    Your feathery nudity would hit a cloud and stop.

(I couldn't reach out.)

V

> O word transformers!
> You stopped giving news from above.

VI

> Sentences are being destroyed…
>
> The world belongs
> To ovals and circles!

VII

There is no world, except in sentences.

the book / the work

THE BOOK / THE WORK

I

The book is the reason
The work exists.

II

The work is the name
of enmity.
—Damned shroud.

III

Every book leaves emptiness in its wake.
One day it will be filled.
(Presence secretes emptiness.)

IV

The work is an attempt at death.
(The book endures all its forms.)

V

The work shoulders the question, not the answer.
The question carries itself.

(Erasing.)

VI

The name in a book
Is a face.
My face, my eyes, my hands.

VII

Each time, the work creates by destroying itself
Though it's written, it's unwritten.

VIII

The book lives through its words.
Does everything with them: is never settled.
Except for sounds.
(What effects these sounds will have are as yet unknown.)

IX

Eventually the book loses its face.
And then we see.

X

The work is walking wounded.
It's born that way.
—It never heals.

XI

The work's walk is a blind man's walk.
So it moves forward.
Knows not where to pause.
But knows where it goes.

XII

Writing is incurable.
(The incurable: You're my country!)

XIII

The work vomits tension.
The book is equilibrium.

XIV

Words! Words!
The book's foetal lunacies.

XV

The work = Nothing.
Nothing = The work.

XVI

The book wants to be shared.
To be shared is both its creation and its funeral pyre.

XVII

Book that wants the unknown,
Lays claim to unknowing.

XVIII

The work is an open wound:
It never closes.

XIX

No book gives you the feeling it's finished.
But it looks finished.

(We should view it as a domestic issue of the work.)

XX

The work has no bearing on reality.
Reality is the reality of the book.

XXI

Like words, letters (those irregulars) suffer too.
I always hear the sigh of letters.
The letter O lives in oblivion to this.
(But O isn't a letter, in Turkish it's a pronoun. And like all pronouns it doesn't complain about its role,
Because it has no self.)

XXII

The unread work can't exist.
—It can't be a book.

XXIII

The work doesn't end.
(Books even write themselves.)

'Books and whores can be slept with' (Walter Benjamin).

XXIV

The book is open to all forms of destruction;
The book breathes the work.

XXIV

The work
Is a question.
'That slope that looks at the long bow…'

XXV

The book is the future.
The future: Tongue of silence!

HALO

> *A poem that does not promote the meaninglessness of poetry, speaks of emptiness and beauty, and nothing more.*
> GEORGES BATAILLE

What kind of poem is it?
a poem that tells of strange and unusual things
a bare footed poem
an incurable poem
a poem that carries water to houses
a poem that holds the hand of mud
a poem that is the sleeping state of language
a poem walking hand in hand with the devil
a poem that spits
a subversive poem
a poem that waters fields
a poem for those that simultaneously exist and don't exist
a poem for the prophet of doom
an impossible poem
a poem in which someone vomits
a brave poem
a poem that says no
an insane poem
a poem that breaks the law
a poem that tells of a matchbox

a poem that breaks wood
a poem like a full moon
a poem that repairs the roof
a poem you can start to read from anywhere
a hard-working poem
a poem like a cursed cell
a poem that walks alone

a poem of strength
an erect poem
a poem that snores
a poem whose words are poison
a poem with a (slight) limp
a poem like the Great Wall of China
a pervert poem
a poem that crushes the ticks of children
a poem like an iron fist
a poem for every object
a poem like an open wound
a poem that never heals
a poem that is my horizon
a poem of divine inspiration

BASILICA

For you my unwavering bell tower
You my weightlessness for you
For you, you are my covered bazaar my dead end street
For you my sleepless my Chechen fly
For you my twenty-third year
For you my amazon my white skin
For you my trickle of water in the clover
For you my half-night
For you my flowing skirt my bread knife
For you my Gibraltar
For you my mysterious chateaux my Chinese lantern
For you my dropped stitch my safety pin
For you, you are my melancholy
For you my flatfish my baroque violence
For you my morphine cell my sand lily
For you my smooth plain my Mount Ararat
For you, me, the one stuck in the swamp
For you my beautiful Moroccan
For you my nettle tree my lute
For you my oxygen tent my yellow jaundice
For you my Far East
For you my armour-plated unity
For you my blind well my inner court
For you my ignorance

For you my haphazard orchestra
For you my veil my open window
For you my rough terrain my acid bottle
For you my tissue my hypodermic needle
For you my child my incurability
For you my embroidery my rebel cell
For you my gas-tap
For you my unripe silk my waterway
For you my bunk bed my bed on the floor
For you my Cape of Good Hope
For you my wind-blown peak
For you my washing line my short cuts
For you my white bandage
For you my early morning
For you my injured icon
For you my white thorn my woollen sock
For you my afternoon's end my cloudless sky
For you my suspension bridge
For you my twenty-four hours
For you my sickness my open wound
For you my broken water metre
For you my leaking roof
For you my damp paper my dry ink
For you my little checked notebook
For you my Himalaya my drinking water
For you my Chinese silk

For you my Tavern my white falcon
For you my steep incline
For you my black market tobacco my watercress
For you my Alpha Omega
For you my pebbles my "T" square
For you my Crusades
For you my princess of darkness
For you my Sodom and Gomorrah
For you my basilica

LONG LIVE NUMBERS

I

1, is the cold one.

Like letters, numbers are individuals.

Their names are their shapes.
We cannot know or see their contents for their natures.
We can't see

    perhaps
      they
           choose
                      not to be seen,

(they retreat into their inner world) and peer out from there.

If they look at all.

And what is there to see, what will they see?
Isn't the world already too visible?
What's going to change if numbers expose themselves?
Shape is everything.
They've figured this out.
Anyway, no one cares about numbers.
Why should they?
Numbers are perfect.
(At any rate Mathematics is beautiful.)

What more could they want?

Only **1**, is ambitious, dim.
Orders everything as it sees it.
Only it too is deprived of shape:
From up above

                 to down

                                below
                                    s
                                    t
                                    r
                                    e
                                    t
                                    c
                                    h
                                    i
                                    n
                                    g

  it

        knows

                nothing

                        else

Plato, only he, had a special love for **1**.
He never knows where to place it.
Should it surprise us, or not? I don't know.
Maybe he chose it because it's easy to write.
Or else it being vertical interested him.
Who doesn't like things vertical?
Really, how did Plato write **1**?
Perhaps it was enough for him to move his pen tip thus.

Yet if we look at Leonardo da Vinci's handwriting in the Vatican Palace
We see he felt no interest at all in **1**.

For him, **1** is something between existence and non-existence.

Pale, barely perceptible, as if he doesn't see it.
Did he look at it as if it lacked content?

PERHAPS.

1 is vast, especially 'vast' is one.
A book could even be written about **1**.
That may not even be enough.
Not enough, because **1**'s wound doesn't heal.
It's everything.
Above all it's a Theist.
(Who has escaped God?)
It's enough to know even this, isn't it?
But no, Plotinus takes the matter further.
For him, **1** is the son of God.
It's the world's right arm.
And like God it can't be grasped, comprehended with reason.
We can only say what **1** isn't, not what it is.
And not only that:
It's the foundation and pillar of the world.
And I can also say **1** blocks the way of poets.

(BECAUSE)

             WHERE THERE

                              IS BEGINNING

THERE

IS

NO ETERNITY

While **1** pioneers its darkness

2, as if slashing with a knife, divides **1** in half.

1 is a Monist, **2** is a dualist.

And this they will always preserve.

Showing how **2** will rise against the absolute rule of **1**.

And this ought to be very welcome for innocent materialists.

Especially against **1** not counting it at all.

(**OPPOSITES NEVER UNITE.**)

2's hardheartedness comes, for sure, from **1** wanting to bind everything to itself.

Maybe secretly it's infuriated by **1**.

It wants, at least a little, to feel its strength.

Didn't

　　　　　the

　　　　　　　　　first

　　　　　　　　　　　　　assault

on

spirit

come

from **2**?

170

Only **2** wasn't satisfied with this

        alone.   How ve

                                      ry

                                      mu

                                      ch

more it has to say

y

e

t

what could be greater than

c

o

n

t

r

a

d

i

c

t

i

o

n?

That's how it is but **2** still can't bear its pig-headedness.

A destitute.

A hermaphrodite.

Thin. Delicate. Dual.

In fact, **2**'s assaults on **1** aren't entirely incomprehensible.

But there's nothing to be done about it.

And what would it change?

Number is number.

3 is the most beautiful number.
Shape of shapes.
Like no other.
As if
      it is
            inscribing
                      a circle
                                yet

(we might say: two angles lying secretively)

two
hooks
(secret-
ively
too.)

      In fact it's two half-circles: Perpendicular.
(Consider
            the beauty
                    of Perpendicular!)

3's beauty comes not just from its shape: it was born ecstatic.
We might also say it's a moralist (it's not the fault of moral things).
A hedonistic moralist.
It's out there perhaps looking for the well-spring of joy.
It never put on a sour face.
Maybe, then, of all the numbers we can only talk of **3** having a soul.

'NUMBERS HAVE NO SOUL'

Well, **3** has a pleasant nature. That should satisfy us.

But alas, it isn't enough for that secret historian of numbers, dear Borges.

Adding **1** to **3** he carves out a new niche for **3**.

Maybe that's why the life-loving Eskimos love **3** so much.

(In the language of Eskimos there is nothing greater than three, except an enormous

LOT.)

Everything ends with "**3**" and "many".

3 circumscribes the world.

And **3** is the future.

That vast distance!

(Didn't we come to know that distance through **3**?)

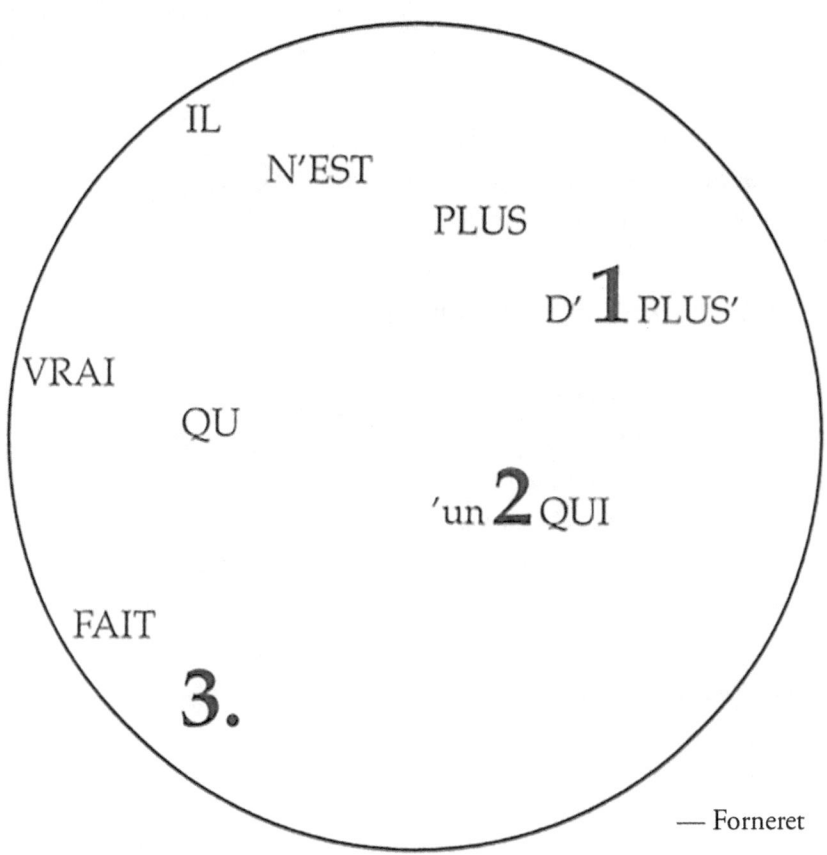

— Forneret

4 is a Kabbalist.

Never dreams.
Apart from Freud, no one complains about dreams.
And what hurt can come of dreams? None but **4** just doesn't dream.
Nor is it ready for life.
(Who is ready!?)
Like **8**, it was raised in confinement.
No one has ever seen it smile.
A stoic: **4** sees everything.[1]
A mere **4** steps from God.
And **4**'s worldview is indexed to itself.
It will learn its place for sure, coming and going.
The road is the road: we've no need to know where.
Closed, inert, unfussed.
As if carved from stone.
An authority, courageous.

---

[1] 4 preaches death and order.

It must be said, it doesn't complain, doesn't grouch.
After all its geography is broad.
It loves its place like pebble stones.
Like all stoics.

Its favourite phrase:

PANTE RHEI[2]

---

[2] Everything is flowing.

5 and 6

are secret numbers. All numbers are in fact a little reticent.
They hide. They close up. From birth **5** is the number of life and love.
Its place in *my dictionary* is completely different. It's equal to the sun.
Thinks itself inseparable from the sun's halo. It's difficult
to understand where it got this from? Like a lot of things
We don't know what numbers aim for in life. Numbers are persistent.
Especially **5**. Everything has its back garden.
5 too. Besides, it's not a crime to love Plato.
Let everyone love whomever they like.

    Let it be a side of **5** we know nothing of.[3]

---

[3] Schiller calls 5 the human soul.

Maybe
 it
  hurts
   it

to
 be
  close
   to
    everything.

6 is a disciple of Hermes. As a number it hasn't had the life it wanted. First it incurred the wrath of old Platonists, and then perfectionist Neo-Platonists.

Thus by adding **1 + 2 + 3**, and by multiplying **2 x 3** was it born. In this way it said nothing about the shape it gave form to and has become

The symbol of what we call perfection (whatever that is). And this bored him.

Perfection is a dead end street. It insisted on disorder, and found happiness there.

In fact, the road it most wanted to travel was a road leading nowhere.

    6 hasn't got used to life.

In the end
                it found
                                truth

by seeking out
           its own
                        loneliness.

'These days I like 7 which stands upside down on two feet.'

7

wanted always to be **1**. But never once thought of the trouble it would bring being **1**.

Did it ever say: 'MY ASHES, DREAM!'?

Let's leave it to the psychologists to resolve **7**'s addiction to **1**'s place.
7 needs no one: it's a rose stain.
But still, I ought to say again that **7** isn't happy where it is.
Of course this has everything to do with it not being valued enough.
7 thinks it's important. As if it was still an undiscovered number.
And it's because of this feeling that it competes with **1**.
It's not enough to be known. It wants to be aloof like a crowning leaf.
And in this it finds success.
7 has many admirers.
Books have been filled.

```
        MB              G
    U       E       I       H
N           R       E               T
```

THE MOST DEVOUT OF NUMBERS

The first in line for heaven. **8** is the garden of gardens.
Right from the start it excludes **1**. Only in God's name
does it pass **1** with each step. It hears it, sees it everywhere.
It's introverted. Never lets out light. It speaks for nothing,
suggests nothing, prefers to keep quiet. So it looks.
For **8**, this is what it means to be devout. But it's terrible
to be silent. Provocative. It has no idea. **8** conveys a feeling
of balance. But here's another truth: **8** isn't easily expressed,
it runs, tears away. This is its personality. And from this point
of view we can call it a Kabbalist. Now that it's tightly closed in on itself,
esoteric, mystical. It's almost impossible to demonstrate
any other harmonious number with such a shape and content.

Always

8^4

chooses difficulty.
The Kabbalistic is such a thing.
(Isn't it easy to be Jewish?)

Lastly: **8** is always hungry and cold.

---

[4] 'I would like to live in the detached two-storey house that is 8.'

9

'IT WAS BEAUTIFUL WHEN THE CLOCK SHOWED NINE'

Dalí is very fond of **9**. He sees it as a faultless example of a cubic picture. **9** is actually esoteric. That's where its centre point is. To **10** (this twin nation neighbour) it claimed the world has no meaning. (**9** sees the world as a heap of shit.)

We've no idea what **10** had to say. But **9** knows that of all the paired numbers **10** is the most beautiful. But it may want to know if this beauty comes of it being the first of the paired numbers, or in being divisible (**10** is divisible like **2**) both in form and content. It might then conclude it views the world in darkness because it is a single number. (Because **9** sees itself as the loneliest of all numbers.) I wouldn't want to recommend loneliness to any number. Numbers are lonely enough as it is. And yet there is something humane in the loneliness of **9**. But I don't know if it's aware of it.

> *'Ten remained behind me, the ten before nine*
> *Not nine but ten*
> *Ten flowers, ten suns, ten Junes.'*

10 symbolizes perfection, wholeness.

10 has a huge world divided in two: Light, vast. But when we say light, it's not everything, there's obscurity too. It can hardly be said the world has saved itself from openness, from obscurity. It's the incurable seed within us! Didn't things (the world we call silent) also take their share like all of us? The world we call silent calls out for parentheses: That's to say, nails, wheels, dusty roads, chairs, stones, windows, notebooks, pens, coal sacks; that's to say, whatever holds the poet's hand, all of that… And only poets? Do they not also tie the knot of reality?

Everything aside, **10** is the happiest number in the world. The thing we call life is **10**.

What about zero

All numbers live at rakish speed.
Especially zero.
The final demon!
The last discovery !

Hey,

Zero screams, saying *'I'm not a circle, I'm a zero.'* [5]
It has a right, throughout heaven and earth. The source
is the source. And who would want that confused?

It didn't fall from a tree: like **1**, **0**s discovery—which required
only one step—has been a gigantic journey. While **1** is held
in great esteem, a leader, **0** is the last great discovery.
And because **0** never once lost hope in the future, the length
or brevity of the future never bothered it. Maybe that's why
it is the language of the future. And of this let no one be in
doubt: because the future is for all of us. And perhaps
it's only the future that cannot be taken away from anyone.
Again only the future can be given out and shared. This
isn't something to sniff at. It isn't satisfied only with the future.
It goes beyond it. Inscribes velocity.
Enormous speed:
It says 'Consider the velocity in multiplication, in growth!'

---

[5] Plato didn't know zero. Neither did his disciple.

great

Whichever way we look at it, both in terms of shape and content,
zero has no equal. As a shape, it's the shape of itself: it takes everything
within: it is everything. It never wavers. To give a name to everything,
it is everything. An identifier. As contemporaneous as it is extant.
Longevity is in its blood. We might say longevity is its self.
With Al Harizmi's help, it reached all the way to now.
How else could we explain it?
An alien.
Fearless!

marathon runner

Compared to 1 (zero is an earthling, it chose the world)
it doesn't cling to God. Again unlike 1 it doesn't exile itself
by climbing walls and ramparts trying to lay claim to everything.
And 1 should understand that it's time has passed. It should
leave God alone. It should recognize zero as the leader of a new
age and retreat into the shade. Zero is the world's new Maestro!
The great chorus!
The language, of enlightenment!

                                                            symbol

And

        which

                number

                                                            of absence

assumes

            both

                        endlessness

and

                         abundance

and

                  finitude

I've read zero is a number that consumes all

II

we entreat with numbers: call out to 1, call out to 2

Numbers came into the world, the place we call earth
(whatever that is: lands, seas, gulfs, headlands;
whatever there is: children, men, cars, women,
horses, death, immortality, rivers, trees, plains)
to measure, to put it all in order. And so
they became the corner stones of our world.
They were born dictators, authoritarians.
2 x 2 is **4** all over the world. This
dictatorship, this harshness they carry
to the end. What about their greed? They
don't know what it means to be sated. Most
of all **10**. (Which has always had respect.)
Ruthlessly ambitious. The same for **100**.

(**100** is brave.) And **1000**? Is it easy
to be a thousand? It should know
where to stop, right? No, it goes on: millions,
billions, trillions, quadrillions, quintillions…
Its greed is boundless. But let's not think
this comes from the nature of numbers. Let Karl
Weierstrass say as often as he likes
'God created integers and we created the rest'.
Even if true, we can hardly say we deserve it.
Numbers don't believe in equality.
They're silent before the inexorable
spread of inequality across the earth.
(Euclid, good old Euclid!)

In fact no one gets on with numbers.
Numbers are a young man's game.
Played only in youth.
Newton found gravity aged **24**,
and orbital motion at **37**, and
gave up mathematics at **50**.
Galois died at **21**, Abel at **27**,
Ramanudan at **33**, Riman at **40**.
Numbers aren't reliable.
They drive us crazy.
They curse and incite us.

So it is, but we can't do without numbers. In particular
we can't do without counting.
Counting is one of our most complex notions.
A huge discovery. In this way we kept
track of the world. And only kept track?
That's how we laid claim to the world.
Everywhere numbers hold our hands. Open or
closed we enter into all kinds of relations with them.
And we don't know why some numbers broker death:

4

is at the forefront. (And some numbers live under great
compulsion; **4** is one of them.) And numbers aren't
alone in their reference to death. It's expected of
everything. (Numbers are the most harmless of things.)
After all, maybe it's in the nature of some numbers
to spread goodness, evil too.

We know, numbers know no end, they go on producing meaning:

3 + 5 = 8

that symbol of love which for us means everything. Number **5**
too implies colour (numbers are known to be colourless).
7, imagining itself on Mount Kaf, is mystery.
Lined up like terrace houses **1, 2, 3** symbolize harmony, melancholy.
Terrific harmony.
6 believes it is damned.
10, lover of lovers, fell from the sky and is perfect.
And then **9**, smelling of excess reason.

And every number has a voice:
1 is shrill; **2**, scary; **3**, angry; **4**, ill-tempered; **5** is cold; **6**, cursed;
7, crazy; **8**, sorrowful; **9** is wild; **10** is magical.

We make numbers do what we like, and we use them
as we like, but they cannot be grasped like an apple.
They are, and yet they can't be. It's not easy to understand.
(Nothing is easy.) Counting is an operation. But
no number can be counted without being singled out.
After 1 we say 2, and saying 3, 1 is already left behind.
Where it goes, and why, no one knows. Numbers
and letters (voices aside) speak the same language.
But still they can't understand each other. We expect
from numbers what we expect from sentences.
Wherever the sentence takes us, numbers take us there
too. Numbers contain questions and answers. (Numbers
are not without them, like nature.) They rain
down questions on us. Most of all:

How Much?

As if their very existence depended on it; they ask and then
retreat. Their comings and goings almost form a secret history.
The reason is an unknown affair. Like love. We know
little of the relation between Yahya Kemal and numbers, except
that he hated the Arabic numbers most of all:

This much we know. When he comes to the **6**th page of his manuscript *Aziz İstanbul* he quickly sketches over it.

It looks anything but like a **6**. As if he hadn't counted it. And he's not entirely unfair, given how **6** is a little dim and severe. Poets aren't so tolerant either. He takes exceptional pains over **7** and **8**. He's not satisfied just to carefully write them down, he puts a circle around them. In fact, we can say the same for **2** and **3**; he circles them too but neither gets enough attention. Montaigne gave particular attention to **8** and **9** in his handwriting, and wrote the two most beautifully of all.

And Baudelaire made 7's leg as long as he could. As if 7 gathers up smells and colours for him. Only scents? Lust too, of course. The same goes for all revealing numbers. And where isn't there desire? All numbers unsettle me, me the feeble. (Despite my love for 3.) Open numbers believe in Euclid. Their lives are open to Euclidian equations. (Numbers inhabit a world of their own making, and they ought to be forgiven for it.)

In the handwritten manuscript of *Piyale* Ahmet Haşim shrouded himself in concealed numbers. It shouldn't surprise us. Introversion and the unknown are what poets struggle with. Regrettably we know nothing of Fuzûli's and Bâki's interest in numbers. Nor Neşâti's—that hidden spring. Perhaps he loved 3. I'd like to know what he thought of it. What a terrible shame! It's easy to count numbers quickly, but not easy to write them as they deserve. And of all the numbers, after 4, 7 is the most difficult to write; 7 requires care. I write 2 the best, and 5.
(And 5 knows it.)
I sketch 2 with a quick flourish...
Like this:

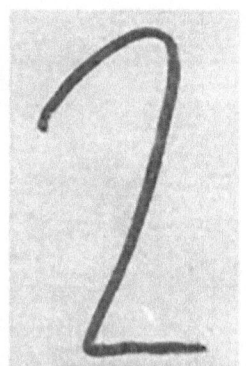

So two was the easiest number to find.[6] Like subtraction, **2** is Etruscan. (Etruria! Few words are as magical. Its entire magic comes from its remoteness.) In finding **1**, of course, (**1**'s place is in ascendance) **2** finds its geographic bearing. **2** is found easily through its own striving. Why should we make things harder? **4** makes us work the most. You find **IV** by subtracting **1** from **5** (**V**). But not for this alone is **4** difficult; above all when we compare **4** to the others, it's the most difficult to write. It's not enough merely to twice raise the hand, you have to draw a proper triangle. And then **4** can't bare the presence of **5**. In fact, never in history could numbers stand each other. They do whatever they like.

---

[6] 2 doesn't know that it's standing, does not fall because of its balance: It thinks it's God-given.

We use numbers and yet there's no escaping their yoke around our necks. Like everything else, they lay claim to the earth as their own.

They are ready everywhere. Poised like shadows at one remove from the things they name.

The absolute value of numbers is the value they carry over and above their symbols.

They aid and name objects, but never describe or designate. They only imply, imply and withdraw.

In their eyes a telephone directory has absolutely no meaning at all.

And it's the same with pain, joy, death (yes, even death).

When they come together on a list of lottery winners they haven't a clue what it all means.

300 Million: Winning Numbers!

```
0006946  1498785  2972247  4157706  5241607  6665142  7862751  8946803
0007809  1555222  2999397  4164733  5259680  6681708  7926223  8949457
0015642  1573635  3014988  4209061  5267175  6687596  7976617  8976809
0100708  1587849  3029379  4228194  5312555  6705490  8018846  9015222
0160067  1664585  3046001  4239263  5389367  6705847  8050913  9111438
0169203  1709320  3071164  4275183  5512667  6753090  8075165  9143836
0172526  1717921  3105345  4276324  5514806  6759604  8090191  9159867
0261903  1747877  3123272  4331890  5534286  6778502  8186520  9193400
0293177  1773707  3188338  4366042  5545011  6783243  8234926  9236037
0321058  1825095  3228938  4401810  5552250  6800746  8305285  9244208
0322098  1829037  3291201  4411780  5569910  6817427  8384619  9263706
0347052  1881553  3293789  4413296  5578854  6878934  8389969  9269853
0365333  1908598  3343978  4427023  5662323  6891526  8390894  9291308
0365487  2046662  3374725  4458101  5670999  6894817  8409031  9292732
```

Two apples plus three apples equals five, but numbers don't know apples.

2 + 3 = 5

For them counting is productive.

1 will go and stop next to a lone precipice beside the sea; **2** next to two trees; **3** next to three hills; **4** next to four tress; **5** next to five children; **6** next to six women; **7** next to seven men; **8** next to eight horses; **9** next to nine cars.
And so each number will assume its form.
Apportioning, moulding meaning. Stirring up the world.
(What you call meaning even threatens the wise.)

Numbers should circulate with the wind.

III

this number has the nature of a Brahmin

Numbers coexist with their shapes.

When lover of lovers Pythagoras (it's said Pythagoras never touched a pen) held the hand of numbers, they became one of us.

Nor is it true they suffer being strangers.

Numbers' past—for past is a problem for numbers too—is blacker than black.

(What is luminous?)

And
        the past
                is the name
                              of darkness

Numbers
              took
                              their share
                                                    of it too

88

Eight symbols have been used to write this number. And that's not so for all numbers. **3** wasn't any trouble. Whatever it was before is what it is today. No one is surprised by this. **3** is like **8**, audacious, an entrepreneur. (**8** is known to be audacious. That **8** is audacious is very dubious: one cannot stir it.)

Numbers incur the wrath of form. And so some numbers are open, some are closed. Why they should be open or closed, no one knows. Form and content are inseparably bound: Maybe that's why.

In the hands of mystics—these loners of the lonely—numbers change shape constantly. Especially 7^7, for no matter how we look at it, it's a mystery right through to its bones. Like God—well almost—it wants people to die.

(GOD IS THE NAME OF DEATH.)

3 was raised in trios. We see it everywhere. And the world is three-dimensional. **3** is everything. It surrenders its identity wherever it can. It's malleable. It's the first number to play the role of a geometric shape. Time has three-dimensions too (past, present, future). Space too (length, height, width).

3 plays a hand in everything. The prophet Jonah spent three days in the whale's belly, Freud didn't know where to put **3**. He proclaims it a masculine number (in the shape of a cock). **3** symbolizes Dante's *Divine Comedy*.

---

[7] 7 is the childhood of man.

5

5 = Swollen River.

Teslis: Baba, Oğul ve Kutsal Ruh, *Saatler Kitabı*, tahta oyma resim, Paris 1524.

9, like **3**, gets in everywhere too:

Jesus died in the ninth hour of the day; dear Odysseus journeyed for **9** years; Plotinus wrote Ennead in **9** books.

And **9** pioneered the search for Plato's age of death:

$$9 \times 9 = 81$$

Poet of poets e.e. cummings (who always wrote his name in lowercase) is never slow to exalt **9**:

Feet walk for each mile
And the heart goes 9.

In the past people weren't satisfied enveloping different meanings around single numbers, they took them all the way from **10** to **10,000**. For some reason they looked with particular suspicion on **10** (the most loved of Ovid, and incidentally our fingers).

It's largely because **10** is the first paired number. And doubt is open to everything.

According to Plato paired numbers are flowers of evil. Shakespeare will overlook paired numbers and say that single figures are divine. But this isn't going to change a thing.

10 accepts everything. Pythagoreans find it divine. So it is, **10** will knock at the door of a new abundance. And thanks to Aristotle books will be written in **10** parts. We'll learn that the world was created with **10** words. Kabbalists will thrust **10** before us everywhere.

A lot has settled on **10**. Its shadow stalks every page of *Zohar*, that book of books. It's there in all manner of senses.

In finding **10**, **1** is given every chance (**1** is never sated). And it brings forth numbers similar in kind. Down falls number **11** as if falling from the sky. That great scientist of numbers Petrus Bungus will interpret **11** as the number of sin and redemption.

Number is never slow to take its place. It chooses sky because it is a Zodiac number; but it never stops shooting its arrows to earth. The symbol 12, is the symbol of 12 Gods. 12 fascinated Dürer, on a map he made in 1515, not forgetting the 12 winds which move the earth.

People have adored 12.

It's a warm number, 12. So it has come to be known. Which just shows how easily it has been accepted.

Number 13 always unsettles us. It raises the question of whether it brings good luck or bad. And so it comes to be known as a negative number. Annemarie Schimmel writes how fearful Napoleon and Roosevelt were to sit at a table of 13. Basically, 13 is a number from hell. And yet Kabbalists view it as a lucky number. We can't easily explain the symbols those numbers acquire on earth. The earth can't live without legends. Man can't do without giving meanings. It's his job.

13 is at the forefront. Like a God, it looks as though it will drag the world along in its wake.

Numbers **14** and **15** envelope the moon. The full moon is **14** days. The Hurufi's unite the human face and body with **14** using the mysticism of letters and numbers. **15** is the holy number of Ishtar. Nothing escapes being holy in the hands of the ancients, and **15** is no exception.

16 is a symbol of measurement, wholeness.

4 X 4 is with the Rosicrucians.

17 is conquest; **18**, chaos; **19** is the moon; **20** is the base of counting.

Number **21 (7 X 3)** is multiplication, magical.

Symbols, rumours, allegories never leave numbers alone. Numbers have been exposed to Platonism, Augustinianism (closed experiment, metaphysics), and are almost pushed out of their nature: especially **40**, as if it resembles wholeness, not **40** apples; number **50** recalls only regret, and not Hesiod's **50** trees or the **50** cattle of Hellos. So it is, but it wouldn't be wrong to see them as upstarts: they change everything. Nothing is impossible for them. Neither light nor darkness too.

*I took cruel pleasure thinking about number **13***.
Marcel Proust

These multi-digit numbers couldn't stop themselves meeting with the symbols in my private dictionary.

99 The **99** beautiful names of Allah.
100 'Let the Hundred Flowers Bloom.'
101 Atlas of Darkness (which is horribly sexual).
102 Pandora's box (that fears for its life at night).
103 Postman of the East (the poem's long horizon).
108 Titivilus (that classic under the pillow).
120 The Angel of Death (the seventh stratum of suffering).
144 St. John's dear number (adorning the skirts of Mount Zion).
153 Is loneliness, History.
216 Is the Golden Oriole with three souls.
300 The great leveller (is the sick-house of **300** blind).
432 Station of Transitions (is surrounded by hanging gardens).
440 The Hell Readier.
441 Maria Magdelena (the revue girl, a child-woman).
1000 The Auditor of Death.
1001 Wounded Eros.

Take the numbers from everything, they will all rot.
Isidoré

Nothing escapes form. Because form is everything. Numbers are the same. Is being such as small thing? What more could be wanted? Painters are the first to recognize numbers for their shapes. And the first of them was Magritte.

Magritte loves playing with numbers. He had a casual interest in mathematics. Everyone has a way of doing things (in their own fashion).

Le Logicien mathématicien de René Magritte

But only him? What about the guy who painted them

                        Pop artist

             Jasper   Johns

      who   painted

  portraits   of **1** to **9**

but   somehow

left   **0**   out

neither   its form

nor   content

  interested   him

    considering it   perhaps

      midway   between

         existence   and

                 absence

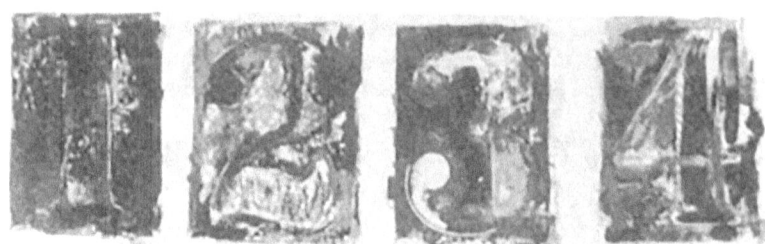

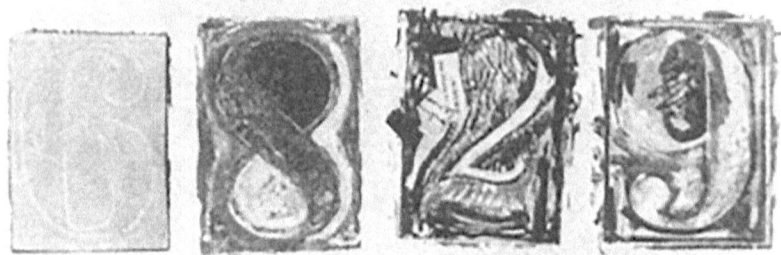

And 'absence' is an act much like zero. Emptiness
is fullness too. We shouldn't be afraid but just
go along with it. Jaspers ought to know this too.
0 should be put in its place. Above all
we ought to extract the magic of zero.
Because zero *is* magical: it spreads magic.
Any time, any place there it is before us.
And who can do without it?
Perhaps he never saw **0**, and knows nothing
of it. Why not? Besides, zero isn't a
number, it's numberlessness.
But from painters we learn to look
at numbers as though they were pictures.
Otherwise we'd just say numbers are numbers.
For example: before Franz Kline
the number **8** was no different
from any other number. Through him
we saw **8**'s enchanting beauty.
And we hung it on our walls like that.
Numbers haven't escaped the painter's
hand. So the abstract world of numbers
became ever more our world.
But still something is always missing:
Their voices! ('Their voices
are the semblance of being')
No one has wanted to know their voice.

It's still the same.

Franz Kline

We see numbers in every age. Not satisfied just to walk in tow with the world, they founded and wrote new geographies. Not even they could escape the wrath of history. In the hands of ancients they grow lunatic: they give wings to elephant armies, small villages, houses, women, barbed wire, child-suns, rocks, kites; trains, waterways and airways—they made them all. And nowadays they make someone like J.M.G. Le Clézio write deathless poems (by collecting numbers from the ground and placing them one under the other as if they were words):

$$
\begin{array}{r}
065 \\
150 \\
1000 \\
590 \\
250 \\
045 \\
600 \\
825 \\
075 \\
060 \\
175 \\
320 \\
400 \\
750 \\
095 \\
\hline
5400
\end{array}
$$

Numbers have a long life. No one knows their future.

It's not hard to see why they take various forms. Single figures have always been liked.

God loves single numbers too.

1, 3, 5, 7, 9

how

l
o
v
e
l
y

Some

            numbers

                        are open

some

numbers

are closed

$$\begin{array}{ccc} & \mathbf{6} & \\ \mathbf{5} & & \mathbf{7} \\ & \mathbf{9} & \end{array}$$

These are the most beautiful of the open numbers.

Especially **5**.
(**5** = swollen river.)
It's clear, whatever it is.
Clarity is sensual, it takes over you.

9 is the last of the single figures. It opens a world to those numbers that come after it.

It is as if it were the very name of enlightenment. It's open to dialectics: at least, it doesn't object.

6 and **7** are difficult. They are there for difficulty. This alone might have made them known. Numbers are our private witness. The lack of one upsets the other. They line up from **1** to **10** but that doesn't mean '**3**' proceeds '**4**', or that '**8**' follows '**7**'. And we can't say '**3**' is somehow earlier than '**4**'. Heidegger will have none of it, saying: "Numbers are non-temporal and cannot be either early or late." But this is also true:

Space & time

                are numbers'

                                forms

outside

                their

                                form

      they have

                no other

                            sense

Numbers are a forest of symbols:

1/ Is faceless.
(Second-hand birds, insects, children)
2/ Innocent moralist.
(Long hair, long nights and unwound silk)
3/ Virgin Mary.
(Blood, Aztecs, forests, water's memory)
4/ Other worldly.
(The repressed, shoved aside, flat-footed)
5/ Passionate love.
(Djinns, elephants, gold inspectors)
6/ Distant shore (melancholy)
(Netters, diviners of water, bees)
7/ Colour blind.
(Undreaming, days wondering around)
8/ Monist.
(Hairpins, yellow buttons, white scissors)
9/ Reticent love.
(Idle rivers, those living near their banks, misty mornings)
0/ Auto "I" (sorrowful)
(Ants, aquatic flies, goat tracks)

We would never know numbers, if they weren't such exposed entities. Their lives, their identities are indebted to counting. Suppose we never hold their hands, it's as if their very existence were thrown into doubt, they don't reveal themselves and turn around and around in the same place.

Numbers live inside everything, and outside too.

They assume a shape, but do not move from one to another.

(Everything has a dilemma; theirs is this.)

Some intellectuals have been fascinated by numbers.

Chief among them, Aristotle.

Secretly he likes **1**, but he only touches it lightly and doesn't take it on (**1** has seven souls, like the number **7** too, so let's forgive it here). Perhaps it doesn't want to be overly familiar with God (God forces us to talk about him, and he loves it). And we can't prove **1** with reason, nor refute it. (**1** says it comes from the same race as Thales; and like Thales, it sleeps with water, wakes with water.)

And this is also a truth: that we cannot set out without **1**, for if ever we do, we stumble. And in repeating **1** we find **2**, which is everything. Everything, because it opens the way before us. We are indebted to it for our intimacy with life today.[8] And we can't think without numbers, we can't even do the simplest thing. (Here is the perfect place to make the thinker's ears ring, for without them we couldn't even approach numbers. Foremost, without Kant. These days they spare precious little time for numbers. Dear Hartmann [they say his bed is in his paternal house] is interested only in the living—only them—and knows nothing else. Kierkegaard, Husserl and Heidegger opened parentheses only for "being". Perhaps they wanted me to come and explain it all, so the pleasure I take in it is my right.)

---

[8] 2, sees itself as a tree-lined street.

summation

I don't know if we're too late to say: Numbers
are Pythagoras' burden. Perhaps that's why he never
found time to discourse on death (is there a single thinker
who doesn't talk about death?) Perhaps because of his fear
of death he held fast to numbers. And if you ask me, your humble servant,
it was enough for me to know that numbers are only from the world of
things.
The silent world always keeps me happy. Moreover,
I see myself as a member of that world.
Especially where numbers are concerned. Who doesn't like
numbers? I look at numbers from **1** to **10**
as if looking at a picture. I find great beauty there.
And I've been passionately tied up with some numbers.
For example, **3**. I've been interested in **3** right from the start
but it's something I can't explain. It's more of a physical thing.
It's difficult to explain too. But I can say this:
we're like each other with **3**. **3** is an island.
Like me. I suppose we are the same age and size.
Whenever I think about **3**, I assume I think about myself.
It's fragile and thin like me. Basically, it's pessimistic.

Perhaps I like the pessimism in **3**. It's indulgent,
a disciple of Hermes. And then it's an experimenter (like me).
And also like me, it's immanent, introverted.
3 isn't usually liked. Not even Mohammed looked warmly
on **3**. But that was his choice. It doesn't kick and scream
like **8** and **9**. And doesn't always want to be in the lead
like **1**. It's modest, hardworking. It believes in love.
(What else is there to believe but love?) And has no time
like a stream. Beautiful like a sleeping water. Bird
voices never missing from its inside pocket. Then
it's surreal. It's bent like a shape (there's nothing better
in the history of the bend). Haste of haste: An adolescent! All
embracing, egalitarian.
And like all good poems it stirs up feelings of guilt.

And I like **5** too. **5** is the sky's rainbow.
It's concrete. And like **3**, **5** engages a shortened life.
The truth is: Why should it prolong it? The ancients
counted to **10** only to start back from **1** once
they reached it. I also know how to count to **10**
and once I reach **10** I too start over again
from **1**. **10** is enough for everyone, with more besides.
We could even have stopped at **5**.

It has been said that the world of numbers
is closed, fatalistic. But this is not beyond seeing
Pythagoras' world as the world of numbers.
Numbers are what they seem. Neither more, nor less.
The essence of things is number. And it's through them
that the world is made known. Numbers
are everything. The world is a number.
Reality is a number. Numbers are the vanguards
of eternity. Exalted
eternity!

L
 O
  N
   G

       L
        I
         V
          E

N
 U
  M
   B
    E
     R
      S

HOUSE

house
I

> *With Usura hath no man a house of good stone*
> *Each block cut smooth and well fitting*
> — Ezra Pound

Wall
Door
Window
+_____
HOUSE

I

Our subject, you gather, is house.

So, we're going to wander around in the world of things (by world we mean no more than "the world of things"). And this world we know too. It is, therefore, enough for us to open a dictionary (dictionaries are the embryos of life) and to list the things we see. Everything there is arranged and neatly set out with great care.

(Isn't everything scripted anyway?)

Ambulance	Ebony	Monument
Avenue	Flag	Mosque
Azalea	Garden	Net
Babel	Glass	Opium
Baghdad		Pocket
Broad Bean	Glass-eyed	Sack
Chimney	Green Plumb	Sage Leaves
Circus	Gumbo	Showcase
Cloak	Island	Spices
Conjunction	Jacket	Tent
Copper	Juniper	Tree
Courtyard	Lampshade	Vineyard etc…

So let's get ready to read these. Didn't the house indeed come forth that we might take its hand for such a journey?

Anyway, to reach out and grasp at the outer edge of things is to be in the world.

II

A rectangle (is there a place the rectangle doesn't go?).

We can say a cube too. Every face square, fixed, silent.

A closed box, and like all closed boxes: introspective, closed.

Walls, doors (opening to the unknowing), stairs, windows (seeing what we don't see);

Rooms (dream producers), sofas, beds (our spirits' excitable dukes);

Balconies (predators of space), chairs, cupboards, tables;

A water bucket cast aside, a bread knife, a pin (as a pin);

Medicine bottles, a pair of scissors, open-mouthed, innocuous (why open-mouthed?), a pencil (writing's slave);

Children, thrown, throttled clothes;
And a leaf (as a leaf);
A broken-necked word: Samarkand (visited, to live or to die there);

And an earthenware pot, teeming insects…
And emptiness. Fullness.

Coming & going from room to room, from window to window (isn't it to live, as we said, the going to-and-fro from one place to another?).

And the house itself.
House is detail (God is in the detail too).
Silence, little joys, tiny pains, small conversations, aloneness…

All of it, every bit
A transformation of the world's form
An auto-ego.

A labyrinth.

That goes nowhere, opens onto nothing.

a grand metaphor: house
II

House rings instantly at the door of the world's rich images.

*

House: privileged existence.

*

A place to which we'll always come and go: house.

*

House is a grand metaphor: both right beside us, and at the end of the earth.

*

The house is you.

*

House, is your homeland

*

Our name, house.

*

The house has no one.

*

Everything talks at home.

*

Stairs either go up, or down.

*

At home the door is either open or closed.

*

The house is tight-lipped.

*

Language is the house.

House stores time and lives.

*

Narrow paths feed the house.

*

House rolls up balls of dreams: it's the guest at the dream.

*

A great dream: to be at home.

*

House: throne of the unconscious.

*

House is the world.

spirit of the house
III

I

The home's spirit
longs
to be
no one's.

II

Home,
supposes
there is only
itself.

III

In its dream
a
house
revolves
(as) an early evening.

IV

House syllables you
house.

V

House,
the sleeping
soul.

VI

House
is a bigot.

Life at home
is lost.

VII

At home
everything is a burden.

VIII

Home
remains
forever foreign.

IX

When homes
are vertical,

life
is horizontal.

X

Time
is always

at
home.

XI

Home

smells
of apple.

XII

Homes
are insidious.

XIII

In the house
doors
do not smile.

XIV

Home
is a dream.

Take me
houses!

XV

At home
windows
talk.

—Oh windows,
sing your song!

XVI

Home,
my end.

house as a family
IV

door

DOOR

A voice: how many handprints on the door?

How to form the equation
to find the door?
Add, subtract,
or divide?

```
                    House
                    Window
           X
                   ─────────
                    Door¹
```

In the world there is no sovereignty above that
of the door's.
House, is a door.

First door, then house.

It knew this, right from the start. All precautions were taken for this (it being a door).

No matter how, if the house limits its name and its presence, be it limits without doors, there can be no house.

---

[1] 'Doors, open to empty living rooms.'

There is no house without the door.
Everything comes and goes by way of the door.
The door serves none but itself.

Indeed, the door is a commander, a power-monger like the wall; we should accept it for this too.

Everything is asked of me, says the door's heart.

See, a woman has come along and stopped, reached out too for the knocker, was about to reach out her hand.

She sees it for the first time.
What else is she going to do but knit her brows?

Door = house

Has it become a house?

There is no house

The house is to die in.

room

ROOM

The nature of the house is silence.
Rooms, sofas, stairs, furniture weave silence.

THE HOUSE DEMANDS SILENCE.

House is a winding ball of narrow paths. These narrow paths feed it.
It scatters such silence, limitlessness.
Lives everything fully in this quietude.
(This is the single thing that's shared in the house.)

House is the room.

An island.
(In its own state)
a call within.
In praise of confinement, loneliness.

But we always see a house.
The house is in fact the spectator.
Wanders around, as if it's not there.
Opens, closes doors.
In the house everything is there for each other.
(Confinement requires it.)
Only the room lives for itself.
The house has a dream for every situation.
The room is forever watchful.
The room talks about everything.
There's a meaning to everything too.
(Nothing can escape meaning.)

Man is an island.

The room: A world.

window

WINDOW

        House
        Leaf

—

   ——————
        Window

Foresees the solution to every equation.
So then: THE WINDOW
An eye (seeing all inside the brackets).
Partitioning, encoding, freezing still.
An image predator.
Where in the house, it says, is better to see outside?
(Window believes the view is there for itself.)
Its presence too is indebted to absence.
It has grabbed the world before it.
(The window faces forward.)

Is it a child passing by?

'A child's passing!' it will say.

Is it ice cream a woman is coming to eat?

'A woman is coming to eat ice cream'
it will say.

Is it the sun rising?

—Thanks sun! it will say.

But this too will not suffice, it will announce what it sees to the interior; (in any case the interior wants this).

Such is the window, since everything is there for the inside.
—Who's that beating the glass?
—A straying cloud.
—A leaf.

The window is everything.

wall

WALL I

'Mother, must the walls be so high?'

House is something of a wall.

We could say it's something that doesn't move.
But it doesn't stay just by staying still.
It divides, cuts off, closes (closing is its job).
But we don't see, we don't know the wall.
The house is doors, balconies, windows, stairs.
It's the plumbing too.
The wall hides.
Masquerades as a thinker.
Doesn't give itself up.

If we happen upon a wall, it's a door we compare it too.
It too hides itself like a wall.

Wall considers door of its own kind.
A prohibitor, an authority like itself.
Perhaps this is why from the very beginning it never adopted openness.
Sincere, loquacious too like a window.[2]

---

[2] For sure, we shouldn't expect the wall to understand the door. I don't.

In the history of being
(the history of being is a history of imperceptibles) it's as if the wall alone has no meaning.
Right away it reminds us of the house.[3]

Without the house, its being is doubtful.

We should embrace it for this.
Such a presence.

Those in the house
Beware of walls!

---

[3] I ask you, wall, how is it you're indestructible?

WALL II

By its nature, the wall interrogates everything.
—What's behind the wall?
If it's this garden wall, then the garden; if the house, then the house, it cross-examines the house's interior.
So it is, the wall builds its metaphor of secrecy from the beginning.
What's curious too, it does this by driving its curiosity bugs back and forth.
Every wall shoulders this.
And slowly secrecy becomes the walls reason to exist.
For sure, the wall is not aware of this.
It knows nothing of this.
Besides, wall is a house.
It's a house, thus it justifies itself.
Later, it's in the house we more often come across the wall.
But to say that is no more than a hypothesis.
Because we don't see the wall at home.
If we put it like Jacques Peret, we only see the wall when we hang something on it.
And for sure when we bang our heads against it.
And just for a while.
Then we immediately forget.
The wall is secrecy.
Secrecy, the wall's incurable destiny.
It cannot be escaped.

WALL III

Everywhere we're as close to walls as flesh to bones.
When the window, door, balcony, ceiling etc are a part of the house, the wall is everything.
We wander in the house from wall to wall.
But the wall lets no one sense its dominance.
It never opens up without thinking first.
For sure, this too is its virtue.
As with all things, the phenomenon of walls (why don't we say its poetics?) is silence.
It is wounded with silence.
This too it scatters through the house.
A great, enchanted silence.
Open to everything.
The wall grants us this.

The wall is open reading.
Miracle-filled.
(Where aren't there miracles?)
It's enough to read it.
Walls render us speechless.
There's no escaping walls.

WALL IV

Wall is a discovery.
When the house (the house's logos) induces dreams of richness, it's as if the wall excludes itself. It distances itself from everything.
It doesn't share the house.
It behaves as if there were no house.
Only the house?
It doesn't count itself among the towns, the squares, the gardens it encloses and surrounds.
It lives by withdrawing from everything.
It has chosen aloneness.
As windows, doors, balconies, rooms, ceilings and cupboards live together, wall is like the stranger of the house.
It's Penelope.
Nose to the ground.
Doesn't complain, doesn't beg.
In order not to reveal itself it hides its appearance; throws away, cleans out all of its corners and outer edges.
Its power too (the dominance of a wall) it reduces to zero.
It can't be said this is what the wall wants.
Who wants loneliness?
Still, it must mean something to the wall.
But we'll never learn this.

Everywhere the wall is alone.
The wall doesn't smile.

Summation

I love all stone walls, especially those at the entrance to roads, I love huge, old, neglected, abandoned stone walls between a shabby, ruined fence. I hear their voices. A vanished, magical world stirs within stones: it calls us to mysterious travels. Stones have no egos, or else there is an I that's wandering. Stones are always stones. (Nothing is complex, unless man complicates it.) I once wrote that I wanted to be a stone mason, a wall builder. Wall masons are happy people. They can see the work they do: they touch, hold with the hand. In Halicarnassos there are wall masons, and walls, I've made friends with. Many of them are stored in my memory. I can't pass one of them without saying hello. I've witnessed walls talk. I've heard their vast silence. Lived through their epic poem. I've run my hand around and over them all. I've idolized them all.

It's still the same.

garden

GARDEN

> *'I'm in the middle of a garden that resembles 444'*
> Edip Cansever

The house, 'vertical presence'.
The house is entered from the garden
But the garden doesn't know the house
(Nor perhaps the house the garden).
How beautiful!

In fact, the world of objects is like this.
They make the most of the unknown.
The garden chose freedom, right from the start.

However much the house makes itself known, it knows how to wipe out the house.

—I am in the garden! It says.

It has its own language, history, geography.

We know too it has some thoughts of its own (it's from these thoughts and no others that the garden takes its shape).

WE SEE THE HOUSE AFTER PASSING THE GARDEN.
If we compare the garden and the house, against the house's inscribed closedness, its conservatism (the house is a dictator, wounded by despotism), the garden is wide open.
IT IS REVOLTED BY SECRECY.

The garden is full of sound.

Its face overflows into the street.

It presents a feminine reading.

If we again compare it to the house, it's sexual (what isn't?).

Garden, mudded singer of the street.

Dirty child.

Hello gardens!

little gods of the house
V

THRESHOLD

I

Threshold
the house's little god.

Thresholds open
to the unknown.

II

Threshold
moving away from home.
(*In the prolonged sky.*)

III

Threshold, is another place.

IV

Threshold
sing your song!

STAIRS

I

House,
said it didn't understand
the language of stairs.

II

Stairs
open to the subconscious.
(*To the full moon's huge brightness.*)

III

Stairs,
the home's
dark presence.

IV

Stairs,
the home's
inner journey.

V

Stairs,
the home's foetus.

CEILING

I

Ceiling
doesn't know house.

(*Supposes itself the house.*)

II

Sky,
the house's ceiling!

III

Ceiling, sky's
dream haunt.
(*Overflowing sky's.*)

IV

House,
pretends not to see
ceiling and roof.

ROOF

I

Roof
always breaks
the house's
dream.

II

Roof,
the house's
spell-craft.

III

Roof
walks
with night.

BALCONY

I

Balcony,
thinks itself the cosmos.
(*The Little Phoenician.*)

II

Balcony,
children's hanging spirit.
(*Balconies should walk with night.*)

III

Balconies,
the house's eye.

IV

Houses
never did understand balconies.

V

Balcony,
the house's alcoholic child.

NOTES

O Diligent Like an Apple: Arif Damar (1925–2010), prominent Turkish poet.

Golden Oriole : Enis Batur (b. 1952) is a prolific writer of poetry, essays and criticism. His *Selected Poems*, in English, is published by Talisman House.

Identity Book, Unbelonging : Mustafa Irgat (1950–1995), Turkish poet. His book *Ait'siz Kimlik Kitabı* (from which Berk borrows the title) won the Arıburnu Poetry Prize in 1995.

? : Yahya Kemal (1884–1958) and Ahmet Haşim (1884–1933) were two of the most influential neo-classical poets of the early twentieth century, much influenced by *divan* poetry and the French Symbolists. Tevfik Fikret (1867–1915): his first book, *Rubab-ı Şikeste* [*The Broken Lute*] was published in 1900.

Neyzen Tevfik : A painting entitled 'Neyzen Tevfik' by the Turkish architect, painter, sculptor and storyteller Cihat Burak (1915–1994). Neyzen Tevfik (1879–1953) was a famous ney player and a hard-drinking Bektaşi dervish, as well as a poet and satirist.

Long Live Numbers : Fuzûli (1494–1556) and Bâki (1526–1600) were two of the greatest Ottoman *divan* poets writing in the time of Süleyman the Magnificent. Neşati (d. 1674), also writing in the *divan* tradition, led an order of the Mevlevi dervishes in Edirne.

A GUIDE TO TURKISH PRONUNCIATION

With few exceptions, where Turkish names appear in the book I have employed standard Turkish spelling. The exceptions are those words for which well established anglicized forms exist, such as *İstanbul* and *İzmir*, which are commonly written in English with *I* rather than *İ*.

As a guide to pronunciation the following may be useful:

a (*a* in *apple*)
b (same in English)
c (like *j* in *jam*)
ç (*ch* in *chips*)
d (same in English)
e (*e* in *pet*)
f (same in English)
g (*g* in *gate*)
ğ (lengthens a preceding vowel)
h (*h* in *have*)
ı (*i* in *cousin*)
i (*i* in *it*)
j (like *s* in *measure*)
k (*k* in *king*)
l (*l* in *list*)
m (same in English)
n (same in English)
o (*o* in the French *note*)
ö (same in German)
p (same in English)
r (*r* in *rug*)
s (s in sit)
ş (*sh* in *ship*)
t (same in English)
u (*u* in *put*)
ü (same in German)
v (same in English)
y (*y* in *yes*)
z (same in English)

www.ingramcontent.com/pod-product-compliance
Lightning Source LLC
Chambersburg PA
CBHW022001160426
43197CB00007B/227